Negotiation

for Health and Social Services Professionals

of related interest

Performance Review and Quality in Social Care
Edited by Anne Connor and Stewart Black
ISBN 1 85302 017 6

Planning and Costing Community Care
Edited by Chris Clark and Irvine Lapsley
ISBN 1 85302 267 5

Boring Records?
Communication, Speech and Writing in Social Work
Katie Prince
ISBN 1 85302 325 6

Negotiation
for Health and Social Services Professionals

Keith Fletcher

Jessica Kingsley Publishers
London and Philadelphia

First published in the United Kingdom in 1998 by
Jessica Kingsley Publishers Ltd
116 Pentonville Road
London N1 9JB, England
and
1900 Frost Road, Suite 101
Bristol, PA 19007, U S A

Copyright © 1998 Keith Fletcher

Library of Congress Cataloging in Publication Data
A CIP catalogue record for this book is available from the Library of Congress

British Library Cataloguing in Publication Data
A CIP catalogue record for this book is available from the British Library

Fletcher, Keith
Negotiation for health and social service professionals
1.Negotiation – Great Britain 2.Health services administration – Great Britain
I.Title
362.1'0941

ISBN 1 85302 549 6

Printed and Bound in Great Britain by
Athenaeum Press, Gateshead, Tyne and Wear

Contents

Foreword

As a professional in health or social services, you will already possess much of the knowledge and many of the skills in this book, and if you are a student social worker, nurse, doctor or psychologist, a significant part of your course will be about developing your knowledge of behaviour and honing your skills in applying it. However, the context is different. Of course you know how to negotiate: you do it all the time. You should not, therefore, regard this book as a whole new body of knowledge to you – if it helps you to refocus what you already know, I will be more than satisfied.

Nobody writes a book like this alone and I am indebted to many friends and colleagues for their insights and ideas. If any of them sees something here that looks like his or her idea it probably is, and I am very grateful! I would like to thank a few people specifically without whom this book would not have been written at all in its present form. I am very grateful to Jessica Kingsley, my publisher, for her help, understanding and encouragement. Several friends and colleagues have 'saved me from myself' and pointed out things which were rash or just plain wrong. Martin Brassington, Alan Coote, Sheila Drayton and Andrew Wood have given me their expert advice on various chapters and sections. Alan Coote and his colleagues in Pi Associates have also generously allowed me to use some of their training material.

A special note of thanks must go to my old friend Herbert Collingham, who undertook the onerous task of reading the whole draft through the sceptical eye of a patents examiner – which he was for the whole of his professional life. His trenchant observations have enabled me to express ideas more clearly and to make the illustrations more relevant than would have been possible without them.

Finally, Felicity my wife has given me many useful insights and ideas. And she did as much as anyone could have done to keep me (or should it be *make* me?) sane during the long struggle for coherence.

For all their help this is my book for which I accept full responsibility, warts and all. If you do find any warts, let me know. I hope you enjoy the book and learn as much from reading it as I have from writing it.

1. An Introduction

What this book is about

Successful negotiation in any context is about four things:

1. being clear what you want

2. understanding the context

3. preparing the ground

4. managing yourself and coping with the encounter.

If you have these four things under control your day-to-day meetings and more formal negotiations will be successful and productive. Although negotiation is a skill, the context in which it takes place has such a heavy bearing on how it is practised that it is almost impossible to acquire it as a piece of generic learning. If you work within the context of health or social services, and want to improve your ability to negotiate, the best way to do it is within that context. That is exactly what this book is about, and as far as I know it is the first of its kind.

Why do we need a separate book about health and social services negotiation? The skills of negotiation are all generic, so why not read some of the general books on negotiation and then apply them to our situation? In fact most of the so called 'general' books on negotiation are not general at all. Almost all of those that are better known have an industrial, commercial or sales slant. *Getting to Yes*, Fisher and Ury; *How to Negotiate Better Deals*, Thorn; *Getting Past No: Negotiating with Difficult People*, Ury; and *Negotiate to Close*, Karrass are all examples of this kind.

Let us look at the last-mentioned to illustrate the point. *Negotiate to Close* by Gary Karrass, subtitled *How to Make More Successful Deals*, is a book written entirely for sales people. The title gives you some idea that this is about commercial transaction, but not that it is simply about selling. If you look at the contents page this becomes a lot clearer: headings like 'How the buyer helps you find it' and 'Negotiating a price *increase*' (my italics) are something of a give-away.

It is an interesting and readable book once you allow for its focus. But some things which are axiomatic in selling are assumed by Karrass to be axiomatic in all negotiation. For example one of his recurring themes is that the more you know about *them*, and the less they know about *you*, the better. The first part of that is certainly true in all negotiation, but the second part depends a great deal on the kind of negotiation you are engaged in. We will explore some of the differences between commercial and non-commercial negotiation later. But one clear difference is that, in most non-commercial negotiation, giving your protagonist a clear understanding of the constraints on your position is a strong bargaining tool.

What negotiation is

Everybody negotiates all the time, consciously or not. It is simply the process of agreeing to do something in exchange for something else being done. 'If I smile at you in a friendly way, will you let me out into the traffic flow?' 'If I get my homework finished, can I stay up and watch television?' 'If you take three kilos of sausages instead of one I can let you have them at ten pence a kilo less.' We practise the art of negotiation every day, but few of us learn the craft.

Is it a general craft at all, or can it only be learned for specific situations? The knowledge base is certainly general and, incidentally, has much in common with a wide range of interpersonal encounters; but it has to be integrated with so much else, which is relevant only to the specifics of the situation, that the skill transfer is not easy. The fact that someone has managed to negotiate a successful joint working arrangement between a GP practice and a social work team does not imply that he or she would be a successful antiques dealer!

In general the questions are always the same.

1. Who am I and what am I doing here?

2. What do I want?

3. What am I prepared to give to get what I want?

4. Who are they and what are they doing here?

5. What do they want?

6. What are they prepared to give to get what they want?

7. How do I prepare the ground?

8. How do I manage the exchange?

9. How do I assess the result?

It is the answers that are different.

Who is this book for?

Negotiating skills are vital for managers, administrators, professional staff, board members, volunteer organisers, commercial service providers, voluntary service providers – in fact just about anybody who works in or with the health and social services. If you work in this field, or have an academic interest in it, this book will be of interest to you.

Formal negotiation forms an increasing part of many job descriptions in the field. Social workers have become care managers. They are assessors of need and containers of demand. They must participate actively in identifying and negotiating for the services which are purchased to meet the needs of their clients. The job will not be well done unless they demand and play an active part in that process.

GPs increasingly control patients' access to health care and, in the case of fundholding practitioners, they negotiate and purchase an increasingly large part of it too. They are becoming the gatekeepers and resource managers of primary and, to some extent, secondary health care. They are being thrust more and more into the procurement rôle, and not just as a result of the increase in GP fundholding: the health service has been broken up into separate provider units, and increasingly the only people who can negotiate with the different limbs of the system on behalf of patients as whole people, rather than collections of symptoms, are the GPs.

Thus, the primary care professionals have an urgent need to develop these skills. Of course the people with whom they negotiate – in the NHS trusts and in public, voluntary and privately provided social care – need to acquire them too.

Finally, middle and senior managers in NHS trusts, health authorities, social services departments, and voluntary and private agencies are engaged in a constant round of meetings concerning planning, procuring, providing and purchasing services. The trend is in the direction of more formalised processes, leading to service-level agreements and exchanged written contracts. It behoves everyone to ensure that what is written down reflects what they believe to be in their own and their patients'/clients' best interest.

In the UK alone, perhaps three quarters of a million people fill posts of this kind or are studying or teaching on relevant courses which lead to these careers.

A changing climate

The direction in which the welfare services have been moving for the past several years has placed more and more activity into the formal negotiating arena. The National Health Service (NHS) has been divided into commissioning authorities and providing trusts. GP fund-holding has been introduced, making GPs purchasers of services rather than merely referrers to them.

In social services the introduction of the 'purchaser/provider split' has put the social worker in the position of needs assessor and service procurer. It has caused most departments to divide at least their community care service into a commissioning arm and a providing arm.

The Conservative Government issued a White Paper (Social Services – Achievement and Challenge, HMSO) shortly before their election defeat. The vision of local authority as a procurer of largely commercially supplied social services is unlikely to survive the change of administration, and was never likely to be successful as described.

The vision which led to the White Paper has already produced major changes. The functional divide in social services and health may have led to greater clarity in some respects, for example, it is now clearer than before exactly what different blocks of money are buying. In other respects it has muddied the water: in the real world it is not possible to make a clear division, in health or social services, between assessment/diagnosis on the one hand and service/treatment on the other. In examining the patient and prescribing medication, the GP is beginning the treatment. In visiting the elderly client in their home to discuss what might best meet their needs, the social worker is beginning indeed to meet them.

All organisational arrangements produce advantages and disadvantages in their wake. Perhaps the major disadvantage of this fragmentation is that it obscures the central purpose. The ultimate intended beneficiary of all these inter-government agency negotiations is the patient/client, and the ultimate accountability is to the public.

The market model tends to disguise this behind the legitimate but limited theory that a negotiation between health and social services, for example, is simply about trading off advantages. In any commercial negotiation one can, in the end, walk away from the table because the deal fails to meet one's minimum requirements; but in the kind of negotiation that takes place between health and social services there is no bottom line. The good negotiator in this situation recognises that there is no bottom line, as all the parties involved have the same major intended beneficiary. Provided everyone keeps that firmly at the top of their agenda a solution must be found.

Old games, new rules

Most people working in health and social services, and indeed many other public servants, regard themselves as professionals, managers and administrators rather than purchasers and marketers. They are often very skilled negotiators with regard to most aspects of reaching mutually satisfactory agreements but, until recently, they have been particularly uncomfortable about the subject of money. Perhaps this is due to British reticence to discuss it explicitly, perhaps it is regarded (only partly consciously) as in some way sordid, but it is certainly the case.

There has been a reaction to this reticence in the growth of the so called 'contract culture'. Informal agreements and *status quo ante* arrangements are no longer acceptable. Agreements covering every last nuance and component must be drawn up and ratified within a process.

In some local authorities and government departments, the starting assumption still is that everything is to be purchased from the commercial sector, and in some cases even the voluntary sector, by 'competitive tender'. This process apes the model of purchase these authorities have employed for many years in the building, construction and supplies sectors. It is in effect an attempt to avoid the need to negotiate by asking people to submit in writing a price for meeting a certain specification and a method for achieving it. To simplify, the lowest price for an apparently credible delivery is then accepted.

The devil in this kind of deal is always in the detail, and there is always such a lot of detail in anything to do with patient or client care. Compare a complex patient/client care procedure like providing residential or nursing care with, for example, refuse collection. If you have ever seen a refuse collection contract you will know that it is a lengthy and complex document with many variables. You may also know that there have been many instances of contractors defaulting on *the intention* of the local authority agreement. But few if any local authorities so affected have been able to achieve satisfactory redress.

The reluctance to include money in negotiation and the recent trend to tendering have had their effect. The quality of the agreements achieved by many local authorities, and the processes they have gone through to achieve them, are often very poor. This is nowhere more true than in the social services, where there is no tradition of buying services 'on the market'. There has always been some degree of service purchasing from other authorities and from voluntary and private providers. It has not been negotiated in any meaningful sense.

The 'price plus' approach to tendering for complex services, in which you go for the lowest price among those who meet certain basic standards, tends to drive down standards in general. You wouldn't even buy a car that way, would you? Fortunately wiser counsels are now beginning to prevail. More forward-thinking authorities are now tending to invite agencies to demonstrate how they would provide the service. Only after the demonstration is there a detailed negotiation, which includes price. It is a lengthier and more complex process, but the authorities are much more likely to finish up with a decent car than a box on wheels!

How to use this book

Part I is in effect a negotiating manual which places the generic skills of negotiation specifically in the context of health and social services. It is designed as a practical tool to give you an overview of the main features of negotiation and suggest ways in which you can practise and develop your skills.

Part II is an exploration of the changes which are taking place in health and social services and their implications for policy, management, service delivery and professional practice. There are also suggestions of ways for managers and professionals in the public, private and voluntary sectors to make use of their skills to exploit the changes to best effect.

Use the sections of Part II you find most useful: those which tell you about the people and agencies you are likely to be negotiating with. I have gone for breadth rather than detail. You should be reasonably familiar with the descriptions of your own services which you find here. But most people will find something in the descriptions of the 'other' agencies which they either did not know or had not considered as to their implications.

Part III gives you a few 'model' negotiating situations to practise on. Use the one which might resemble something as close as possible to your experience in reality.

Use the book in the way which suits you best. I have tried to write it as an interesting read to go through, if you want, from start to finish, cherry-picking ideas which you find useful. Alternatively you can treat it, or parts of it, as a home study course through which you work systematically, making notes and consciously practising some of the ideas in your day-to-day work. You could set up a learning group, with the aid of a training facilitator if you can get hold of one.

Another way to use the book is as a reference tool. You are faced with a situation ahead. Think about the most likely elements of the coming encounter and browse through the contents pages.

Glossary and language

A large section of Chapter 9 is devoted to language differences between health and social services. Three words – constituency, protagonist and she/he – crop up repeatedly in this book, however, and are worth considering separately here.

Constituency

You will find this term is used frequently and it means very much the same as it does in the parliamentary sense. The negotiator's constituency is the people whose views he or she must represent. As well as acting with professional integrity, the public sector negotiator must bear in mind the expectations of his or her council or board, the voluntary negotiator must keep faith with the charitable aims and priorities of his or her agency, and so on.

Protagonist

I have used this word very frequently to describe the person or people who face you across the table, 'the other side'. The OED defines the word as 'the principal performer'. Fowler, in his *Modern English Usage*, defines it, among other things, as 'prominent supporter of a cause', but he rejects the sense in which it sometimes appears: the opposite of 'antagonist'. It does not mean 'one who is supportive of' as opposed to 'one who is hostile to'.

However that may be, I chose the word deliberately to emphasise that the other side is not an antagonist, not an opponent, not a contestant, not a competitor in a battle or a game. The rules of this 'game', if that is what it is, are that both sides should finish up by winning as big a score as possible. There should be no loser.

She/he

Just about the only frequently used class of words in the English language which are gender specific are the third person singular pronouns. This provides a challenge to every author who wishes to emphasise, in the way she or he writes, that everything he or she is saying applies equally to either sex. In order to avoid sentences like the previous one, to avoid overuse of the passive sense, to avoid artificial plural pronouns and to avoid devices like s/he I have simply used 'he' and 'she' interchangeably throughout the book. If a doctor or a director of social services appears as 'she' it does not mean that I think most of them are or should be. It does mean, except where clear from the sense, 'for "she" read "he or she" and vice versa'.

Structure

The book is in three parts. Part I follows roughly the sequence I set out at the start of this chapter:

- being clear what you want
- understanding the context
- preparing the ground
- managing yourself and coping with the encounter.

These divisions are merely concepts; ways of organising your thoughts. The head of a coin is a clear concept, but as a free-standing fact it is meaningless: it must be stuck to a tail. So it is here. Each chapter deals with a concept but, stuck to the back of it, so to speak, are aspects of the other three concepts too.

The broader contextual issues are dealt with in Chapter Three. But we return to the particular context of health and social services in Part II to consider those issues of particular importance to the negotiator in more detail.

Part III contains several simulation exercises, and if you can get a group together I do suggest you try at least the first one. It covers some ground not dealt with elsewhere in the book as well as providing an interesting (and entertaining) learning situation.

I hope you enjoy the book and find it useful and interesting. If you do, and especially if you have suggestions as to how it could be improved, do let me know.

Key learning points

being clear what you want

understanding the context

preparing the ground

managing and coping

A PROTAGONIST IS NOT A COMPETITOR

Figure 1.1

PART I

2. Preparing to Negotiate

Introduction

This chapter is mostly about being clear about what you want from negotiation. Like the question 'What do you want out of life?', this is less straightforward than it appears. If you know what you want you may not get it exactly, but if you don't know, you will not get anything at all.

There was a list of questions in Chapter One:

1. Who am I and what am I doing here?

2. What do I want?

3. What am I prepared to give to get what I want?

4. Who are they and what are they doing here?

5. What do they want?

6. What are they prepared to give to get what they want?

7. How do I prepare the ground?

8. How do I manage the exchange?

9. How do I assess the result?

In this chapter we will be concentrating mostly on questions 1 to 6.

Who am I?

As with all interpersonal skills, the more we know about our attitudes and habits, strengths and weaknesses, the better we function. We also need to know what our job is. People in large public bureaucracies sometimes talk about 'wearing different hats'. Professionals, and others, occasionally experience considerable tension between their various hats.

What is my job?

A county councillor I knew some years ago, used to argue with great vehemence in the social services committee for resources to be found for social services, if necessary at the expense of education. In the education committee, he used to argue exactly the opposite case with equal force. He saw no problem in this. As a member of each committee it was his job to act as advocate for the service responsibilities of each. I often wondered who he thought he was!

However, public servants and many people in other bureaucracies all experience such problems. They are individuals with ideals, ethics and values. They are professionals in the formal sense or in the sense that they wish to do their job with impartiality and integrity. They are the servants of the authority, the board or the minister, and they are accountable for what they do to their line manager, who may or may not see the world as they do. To negotiate effectively, such people must sort out these sometimes competing demands to their own satisfaction.

Attitudes

Negotiation and bargaining have not been a traditional part of the public service culture. Many public servants regard it as slightly sordid and this is perhaps particularly true of the helping professions. Such 'wheeling and dealing' is beneath them. Their vocation and training is for a higher, more altruistic purpose. The signal 'I am above such matters' is a considerable obstacle to the conclusion of a successful outcome.

Some professionals recognise this but over-compensate when negotiating, and do so in the wrong direction. Implicit in their behaviour is the assumption that, in order to negotiate effectively, they must abandon the principles which form the bedrock of their professional identity. There can be few less edifying spectacles than a doctor or a social worker, known and respected for their professional acumen and sensitivity, behaving like a cut-price Arthur Daley. Presumably they think it is necessary to behave like that to achieve their objectives.

There is a great deal of confusion in the attitude of many professionals (and others) towards money, which can cause real problems in negotiation. For many people the subject is taboo and they would rather walk away from a discussion than raise it at all: thus the extraordinary aphorism, 'If you have to ask the price you can't afford it'. Money is usually an issue of some significance in most negotiations and should be dealt with as a matter of fact like any other. In any transaction, if you want something you will be prepared to do things to get it, but there is a limit to what you are prepared to do in terms of time, effort, commitment, and money. If money is removed entirely from the agenda the exchange will be stilted and incomplete.

The opposite tack, that money is the *only* thing which matters in the end, is equally distorting. Beware of over-compensating and watch out for it in others.

Negotiation is the only way to achieve the best outcome for individuals or organisations who need things from each other: this applies to all of us much of the time. It is often regarded as seedy and underhand; a game of shady deals and dirty tricks. It is, or should be, a noble and ethical pursuit. Within the health and social services field it is the way to achieve the best result for the patient/client and it should be entered into with pride.

Competition

Negotiation is often confused with that other modern obsession, competition. Whether you concur with the free-market view that competition is the highest form of human endeavour, or regard it as unwise to invest such energy into creating winners and, by definition, losers, is not the point. From either viewpoint negotiation is an entirely different process.

The salesman trying to sell you a car is not competing with you. He is trying to get you to believe that, in exchange for some (or even most) of your money, you will have a car with which you will be very pleased. You are trying to convince him that you will not buy the car unless he reduces the price to a level you find acceptable.

You are trying to effect an exchange which is attractive to both of you. He is certainly trying to compete with other people who would also like to sell you a car. And, if you are particularly taken with the car, you might be trying to compete with others who may want to buy it. *But you are not competing with each other.*

An unequivocally commercial transaction, in which the objectives of the two parties are exactly the opposite of each other, is not a competition. A non-commercial transaction, where two sides are negotiating for the benefit of a third party, is even more obviously not a competition.

Preparation

Beyond doubt the vital first key to a successful outcome is careful preparation. What do you want? What do you think they want, knowing about them what you do? If you cannot have all you want, what is the least you can accept? What represents failure and how can you avoid it? What have you got to offer them and what alternative offers can you make if they don't like your first one?

How much time, effort and pressure?

The best way to approach your preparation is by making use of a system to help you cover the key issues. Preparation can be a time-consuming business, so the first question to answer is, 'How much time should I devote to this case?' The answer should depend on the scale of the consequences for you, for the organisation you represent and for the clients of the organisation. It should also depend on the impact you are likely to be able to have on the outcome. Theoretically this is, of course, partly circular: the more time you spend the more powerful the impact will be. The reality is that there are some situations which are intractable. You still have to go through with the negotiation – but you know that nothing will change as an immediate result. In those situations spend the time you have available to make sure that you secure the ground for the future. The following example demonstrates what this means in practice.

A senior nursing officer from the health authority, an assistant director of social services and an assistant director of education have come together as a planning team. They have developed a framework for all three agencies together to improve their services for pre-school children on the more barren estates in the area. The research evidence shows overwhelmingly that this is one of the most cost-effective strategies for reducing social poverty and improving the opportunities for children, especially those in deprived communities.

Shortly before they are to present their findings and recommendations to the agencies in a formal meeting it becomes clear that the public spending round for the coming year will hit all three of them very badly. They have received very clear messages that, under these circumstances, there is no possible chance that their report will receive support. They have also had some heavy hints that the tone of the draft they have prepared will be something of an embarrassment to all the authorities and they would be well advised to 'cool it'. How do they approach the meeting? They can:

(a) become more robust and strident in the hope that the case will overwhelm resistance;

(b) let the agencies off the hook of the political embarrassment of having to refuse, by being 'understanding' about priorities and not pressing the case too hard;

(c) put the case dispassionately but forcefully, without giving any ground on its validity, and press instead for it to remain 'on the table' and accepted in principle.

Strategy (a) will probably look hysterical and unrealistic. If there is no money, the authorities are unlikely to shift existing priorities immediately. The case could end up being rejected altogether.

Following course (b) might be the most acceptable option at the time, but is in fact an abdication of responsibility. It is a weak and unprofessional reaction and throws away the case for future development even more certainly than (a). (Incidentally, it will probably gain the protagonists few brownie points in the longer term. It may be recalled by others as deeply unimpressive once the immediate financial panic has passed.)

Strategy (c) may produce some initial embarrassment, and perhaps hostility, but it is the strongest position to take and the best chance of keeping the option open for the future.

There are those who will say that the above example is not a negotiation at all because the three officers have nothing to bargain with. On the contrary, they have considerable resources of skill and knowledge: the question is how best to deploy them. Personally, I do not find it very helpful to see every human interaction as a negotiation of some kind, as negotiation evangelists sometimes seem to suggest. The important point is that much of the preparatory thinking for transactions which are, unequivocally, negotiation is equally valuable in many other situations.

Clarity

Just what exactly do you want from this negotiation? If you don't know that when you walk in the door of the meeting room, you can be absolutely sure that you will not know when you walk out; and whatever it might have been, you will not have got it.

A banker friend told me that people often approach him for a loan or an overdraft without having thought out how much they want. Some of them are not even very clear as to why they want the loan. It seems that they expect the discussion with the banker to clarify those questions for them. If you go to a bank for a loan you do so armed with information about how much you want, how much you will settle for, why you want it and why the bank should lend it to you. If you need to clarify any of these issues to prepare yourself, and you don't feel equipped to deal with the questions, you go to an independent financial adviser.

This example highlights an important issue. Your objectives are not the same as those of your protagonist and you should not expect him to help you identify what they are. His task is to be clear about what he wants. If he has to help you work your problems out you can guess on whose terms he will do it.

Secondary motives

When you come to analyse the likely course of the encounter, it is important to understand what is at stake for yourself and the others involved in the negotiation in addition to the primary and ostensible objective. It is almost never simply the issue on the table alone. As part of the sub-agenda the other negotiators may be:

- Seeking advantage or avoiding disadvantage for the agency or themselves;
- Giving a good account of themselves: 'We did as well as could be expected under the circumstances';
- Achieving a professional objective which may be tangential to the purposes of the agency;
- Gaining (or at least not losing) power or control, not necessarily within the group round the table;
- Gaining profit or avoiding loss;
- Maintaining emotional or financial survival;
- Relieving personal anxiety and stress.

Any number of these things may be at stake for the different individuals. They may not be the same for both sides or even for individuals on the same side. Ostensibly a car purchase is for the advantage of the purchaser and the financial profit of the salesperson. However, it may have all sorts of secondary functions for the purchaser, and it may be a matter of survival for the salesperson if that particular sale is fairly close to some margin below which she will lose her job or her commission. Such considerations will influence the behaviour of each side.

In the case of a negotiation for a bank loan, any or all of the issues in the list might be at stake for the borrower. The banker will need to give a good account of the way he handled the transaction and he will want the satisfaction of doing it well (professional objective). It is unlikely to be about personal survival for him, unless his performance is under particular scrutiny.

It is useful to know about secondary motives, but it is not always easy to infer what they are as they are usually hidden. Here are a few further examples of such motives.

The building is owned by the county. The trust provides the infrastructure in exchange for free accommodation. The negotiation is about how much of the infrastructure is provided by the trust in exchange for how much floor space. An agreement is to the advantage of both agencies. It is a remarkably straightforward transaction. One member of the county team appears to be out of line with the general spirit of dialogue. He is inserting all sorts of apparently extraneous demands and gives the impression that he does not want the transaction to succeed. Why? Because he wants to use the building for something else altogether and that will not be possible if the transaction does succeed.

Sometimes collateral transactions, where the beneficiary is not represented at the table, are ostensibly equally straightforward.

The social services department will provide a social work presence at the health centre if the GPs will provide a peripatetic surgery at a local sheltered-housing complex. Neither party is the direct beneficiary but both assume that they will be able to do a better job, in their own terms, if the arrangement is in place.

There are undercurrents about power and loss of control in the negotiation, and neither side wants to give the other too much of the whip hand. One of the GPs seems to be making a lot more of this than it really warrants. He also seems to want the 'I's dotted and the 'T's crossed in a way which would be virtually impossible in the negotiation itself.

What the social services team does not know is that there has been a major disagreement among the GPs about whether they should go along with this at all. Most of them see it as a good way of meeting their professional objectives, and getting more reliable social work support into the bargain, but the objecting GP does not. There are actually two negotiations, one overt and one hidden, going on at the same time.

There is a further more deeply buried complication in this case. The dissident GP could simply refuse to play ball and have nothing to do with it, but he doesn't feel able to do that. Even though he does not want to be cooperative and supportive, in this case he wants to be *seen* to be. He wishes to be able to give a good account.

It is always important to get your own house in order first. Using a negotiation to bring part of your own team in line is a not infrequent tactic but usually a dangerous one. It can wreck the whole process and, at the very least, produces a less than satisfactory result. If you are not all in agreement about what it is you want, you will not get it.

The following example is of an apparently single and, in principle, simple issue. But there may be many secondary issues lurking in the shadows.

The component agencies of the Area Child Protection Committee decide that their service planning activities entail a lot of duplication and set up a group to report on how they could plan more effectively together.

Advantage or the avoidance of disadvantage for the agencies. The obvious issue: all sorts of benefits and savings could accrue from a successful outcome.

Giving a good account. It is important for the planning group to be seen to seek the advantages. Any failure must be ascribed to inherent difficulties rather than incompetence or inability.

Achieving a professional objective. Doing a good job for its own sake might be high on the agenda of some members of the group, but might be squeezed by higher stakes for others.

Gaining or avoiding loss of power. 'If we lose control of this area of activity by handing it over to them, who knows what might happen?'

Survival or relief of pain. There is a high probability that this will be an undercurrent. Savings usually mean job losses: a happy planner might find himself doing a less congenial job (or no job at all) if this succeeds too well.

Responsibilities and interests

Them and us

'Them' (forgive the grammar) are the people you face on the other side of the table. They represent the organisation to which they have a responsibility. They are also individuals (like you). Some of them may have very similar professional backgrounds and interests to some of 'us'; others may be completely different. Some of them may be close personal friends; some of them may find some of us irritating or even odious. Naturally, none of this will have the slightest impact on the outcome of the negotiation. We are all far too professional for that!

What must they do (responsibilities)

The first thing to address is their responsibility. What does the organisation they represent do? What are its priorities? What will it sustain serious criticism for doing or failing to do? What will it gain kudos from achieving? If you face these questions disinterestedly, the answers you will get will often be rather dispiriting, because they are not the same as the answers which apply to *your* responsibility. By definition, you represent something different with different priorities and responsibilities; there would be no negotiation if you did not. Those are the answers you must address. You are going to solve some of their problems and, in return, they will solve some of yours.

What they might do (interests)

> You are a consultant paediatrician seeking funding from a medical research body on behalf of a clinical team. Across the table is an old colleague and former professional mentor of yours. She is well-disposed to you professionally and very interested in and knowledgeable about the field of study you are proposing for grant aid. She will discharge her responsibility to the research council to target funding towards its priorities and to test your proposal rigorously... But, when she has done all that properly, you can guess where her vote will probably go.

Without breaking any rules it is obviously important to keep people like that as fully informed and supportive as you can; and to do this as early as possible – well before the stage of formal negotiation. Such people will act as your advocates and informal sponsors, although they do not necessarily have to be direct representatives in the negotiation itself. Be very careful not to be seen to be manipulating events and going behind backs: it almost always backfires.

> She is also a personal friend and comes to parties at your house...

Great; but even more need to be seen to be open and above board.

> ...but she cannot stand the senior nurse on your research team: 'that odious little man'.

Keep the poor chap off the negotiating team if you can; keep him in the background if you cannot.

How can we help?

After 'What do I want?' ask 'How can I help them do what they want?'. The answers will be found by reference to their responsibilities and interests. Very occasionally the answers to both questions will be the same. In that case all you need worry about is how to deal with the member of the opposing team who is constitutionally unable to agree about anything. Such people are surprisingly thick on the ground.

Usually the answers to the problems of your protagonists will be very different from yours, even if the ultimate beneficiaries are the same. You are negotiating to solve your problems. *Your protagonists are doing exactly the same thing.* You need to convince them that doing what you propose will make life better for them or – sometimes a more powerful argument – stop it getting worse! The more clearly you understand what they want the better chance you have of getting what you want.

Preparing in detail

Having established the broad parameters – what do you want, what do they want, what might you achieve, how can you help them, how much time is this worth – you need to prepare in detail. You should consider your answers to a limited number of specific questions. I am indebted to Pi Associates for the following planning matrix (Figure 2.1).

WHAT DO THEY WANT?	WHAT DO I WANT? (a) Most desirable outcome (b) Minimum acceptable outcome
THEIR STRENGTHS (What strengthens their case to get what they want from us)	MY STRENGTHS (What strengthens my case to get what I want from them)
THEIR WEAKNESSES (What weakens their case to get what they want from us)	MY WEAKNESSES (What weakens my case to get what I want from them)

Figure 2.1

I find this matrix a useful tool. I draw it on an A5 card and fill it in whenever I am contemplating a significant negotiation. Try it for yourself. Here is an illustration of how it works.

A consortium of consultants has agreed to provide a service to a local authority. No written agreement has been exchanged, but there is a good understanding between them. The consortium has worked for this local authority before.

Then comes a letter from the director of the authority cancelling the £8000 contract. The concluding sentence is, 'I am sorry for any inconvenience this may have caused'. There has been a change of administration at the recent local government election. Using their networks, the consortium discovers that there has been an immediate political embargo on the use of consultants.

The consortium considers that there has been a verbal contract. After some initial reluctance, the local authority agrees to meet two members of the consortium, who prepare a matrix which looks like this:

What Do They Want?	What Do We Want?
To get rid of us as quietly as possible and without any repercussions.	(a) Most desirable outcome £8000. That is what they agreed to. They broke the agreement unilaterally. (b) Minimum acceptable outcome After a long debate we decide that £2500 is the least we will accept.
Their Strengths (What strengthens their case to get what they want from us) The bird in hand: if they do nothing they have got what they want. They don't need us any more because (our spies tell us) they are not allowed to use consultants anymore.	**My Strengths** (What strengthens my case to get what I want from them) Not much except determination and some capacity to make embarrassing trouble for them.
Their Weaknesses (What weakens their case to get what they want from us) They really do not want trouble and they did decide to break the agreement so they may feel their moral ground is not strong.	**My Weaknesses** (What weakens my case to get what I want from them) We do not want the trouble, expense and acrimony which causing the trouble will create. (But we decide we must if we do not get our £2,500.)

Figure 2.2

> On considering the matrix they conclude that, as both sides wish to avoid trouble, that is the issue to work on. They decide to take the line 'If we go for a reasonable settlement it will enable you to go to your committee and point out the trouble we can cause. What we need to agree is the level at which it is not worth the committee risking the trouble'. If both sides agree, all that remains is to decide a settlement figure – which must be at least £2500.

What can we learn from this? The most important thing is the reminder from completing this matrix that this is not a competition. We both want to meet an objective. We are looking for enough common ground to achieve it. We must both win enough of what we want for the negotiation to be successful.

The first few times people use this matrix they usually find it difficult and almost always begin by thinking that it does not apply to the particular case they are dealing with. Persevere! It really does help to clarify your thinking. In the case just described it is easy to assume a one-way benefit, to the consultants only. 'How can we get them to pay up?' It was in reality a two-way benefit or there was no deal: the authority's position being 'How can we stop them making a fuss?'

Key learning points

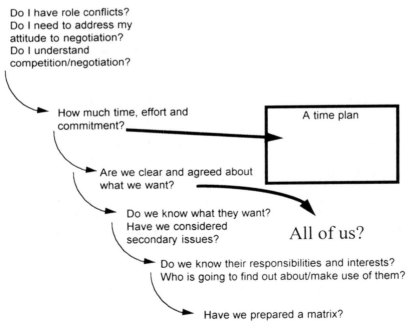

Do I have role conflicts?
Do I need to address my attitude to negotiation?
Do I understand competition/negotiation?

How much time, effort and commitment?

A time plan

Are we clear and agreed about what we want?

Do we know what they want? Have we considered secondary issues?

All of us?

Do we know their responsibilities and interests? Who is going to find out about/make use of them?

Have we prepared a matrix?

Figure 2.3

3. The Context: People

Introduction

One of the axioms of negotiation is: 'The more you know about the person you are negotiating with the better.' How much you enable them to know about you varies according to the kind of negotiation you are engaged in, the people you are dealing with and, to some extent, the kind of person you are. If you think they might use information against you, you will be reluctant to share too much. If you are a naturally open and outgoing person you might find it hard to relate to others while keeping your cards close to your chest. You do need to know about your protagonists. The more you understand about them and their context the better your chances of adopting negotiating strategies which work with them.

The contextual factors

Ask yourself the following questions.

- Do they have a 'professional' agenda?
- Who is watching them; what kind of organisation do they represent?
- What power do they have to make decisions and what must they refer to others?
- What time-scales do they operate to?
- Is their financial agenda constrained by profit and loss, budget or procedure?
- What external factors influence the subject under discussion?

Let us look at each of these in turn.

The 'professional' agenda

In one sense everyone in work wants to be seen as professional: doing the job well and to a consistently high standard. The word 'professional' is put in inverted commas to denote a set of standards which are separate from the hierarchical demands of the organisation, the pressures of the market-place or the individual demands of a particular client/consumer/customer. Our expectation of a doctor is that the diagnosis which she gives should be based on her clinical opinion alone. She does not (or at least certainly should not) ask: 'What illness would you like me to diagnose for you?' or: 'Does the health authority need more or less hip replacements this quarter?' or: 'What diagnosis will produce the best return in treatment costs?' This is obvious for a doctor, whose clinical opinion is often treated with *ex cathedra* reverence. It is equally valid for many other people who work to an externally developed body of knowledge using a set of taught skills.

When negotiating with professionals like doctors, social workers or nurses, you must recognise that their professional standards are an important part of the context. Clever remarks about everything being decided by the bottom line will cut no ice and may simply alienate them.

It is always valid to ask a professional how he reached a conclusion and to engage in a rational and informed debate about it. The best way to make people who are exercising this kind of professional judgement intransigent and defensive is to imply that they do not have the competence to make the judgement in the first place. The professional should be proud of his expertise and will usually be prepared to debate and perhaps amend his judgement; as long as doing so does not imply some sort of concession of professional incompetence.

Who is watching?

Very few people are negotiating in a business or professional arena entirely on their own behalf. They represent a 'constituency'. The line manager's interest will certainly be present at the table, but it is a mistake to think of this in entirely hierarchical terms. A senior person must sometimes take careful account of the views of his staff, particularly if they are collectively held. The negotiators will seek to uphold the primary interests of the organisation they represent but the organisation itself may comprise a number of 'sub-constituencies' of interest.

Thus it is helpful to gain as clear an understanding of the constituency interests which each of your protagonists are representing as possible. You can then present and develop your case during the course of the discussion in terms which will appeal to those interests. If you make clear what they are, you can help the protagonists in the negotiation to present the outcome you have agreed to their constituency. This is important where an agreement has to be formally ratified elsewhere. Even where your protagonists have the authority to agree themselves, they need to be able to justify their decision. They will not reach an agreement with you which puts them in danger.

You should ask yourself why a protagonist is negotiating at all. He may be doing so because he believes the result would be helpful to an interest which he supports, but rather against the wish of his organisation. It may be the precise opposite: he is there because his organisation expects him at least to go through the motions but he sees little value in doing so. Finally, the reason he is sitting opposite you may not be the result of his wish or that of the organisation. It may be due to an external factor (see below) such as a circular advising cooperation, or even a statutory requirement to consult.

If your protagonist does not want anything from you, do you want anything from him? If not, drink the coffee and end the meeting as soon as courtesy permits. If you do want something, you will need to find something that he wants but has not recognised before.

That is not always as difficult as it sounds: people and organisations who wish to function in a bottle, isolated from others, characteristically have very little imagination. Anyone in health or social services who seriously thinks that the two organisations do not need to work in partnership has a real problem. If you cannot demonstrate that they do, then you share the problem! If you are coming from outside the public sector you have to find something it cannot, or for some reason does not wish to, provide from within.

The power to decide

It is always sensible to consider who actually is the decision-maker in any transaction; and it is often appropriate to ask the question directly.

Money

In the case of financial transactions the rule of thumb is that the larger the sum and, usually, the smaller the organisation, the more likely it is that your protagonist will need to recommend to or at least confer with colleagues. A large organisation with clear procedures seldom leaves room for doubt about the formal position and it is perfectly legitimate to ask what it is. Can your protagonist make a unilateral decision about a financial disposal up to a certain sum (always within an agreed policy of course)? Do different procedures apply at different thresholds?

Many organisations do have hierarchical thresholds for the scale of financial decision. Many banks, for example, put a lending limit on their account managers of something like £15,000; on their branch managers of about £150,000; and on their regional managers of £1,000,000. Many local authorities put a spending limit of £100–£5000 (with enormous variations from one to another and even within different departments of the same authority) on their principal officers. Higher amounts can be agreed by chief officers; yet higher amounts by the Chairs of committees; and so on, up to amounts which require a decision of the whole council.

Unfortunately, these formal limits are never the whole picture. They are overlaid by the culture which determines how the controls are exercised. Will the recommendation go through 'on the nod' or be the subject of another, probably hidden, negotiation? How much informal authority and trust does the negotiator have within her own organisation? By definition such matters are never written down. But they can sometimes be discovered through a relationship of mutual trust between the protagonists.

Policy

In the case of policy decisions the picture is complex. You cannot be sure that the person across the table personally supports the line he is taking. On the other hand, something presented as a high level policy decision may actually be nothing more than your protagonist's line. But be careful how you challenge it. Someone may take a line with the *de facto* authority of the agency even though it has not been formally approved. Only if you are fairly sure that the position he is taking puts him out on a limb from the normal position of the agency should you risk a direct challenge. Even then there may be more effective ways of pressing for change.

The policy of an organisation, especially a public one, is always a big issue; but in reality it is often not very clear-cut. It is not unusual for two people from the same agency to take up different policy positions in advance of or during negotiations. This can sometimes be very useful to the skilled negotiator. If you can find a way to reconcile the apparently opposing views of your protagonists, this gets them off the horns of their own dilemma. If it is possible to do so in a way which brings both of them closer to your own preferred option, so much the better; but even if the end result still remains to play for, the rôle you have played as facilitator will have strengthened your hand in the rest of the negotiation.

Practice

In the case of practice decisions, which are an interpretation of law, policy or professional judgement, you can be fairly sure that the decision has been taken by the practitioner himself or someone who works very close to him. In formal terms, the position is frequently that the decision is taken by the agency; but in actual fact, it may simply be a ratification of a recommendation from the practitioner. In a negotiation about practice decisions – for example, a case discussion among professionals – practitioners will usually be able to make agreed changes themselves. However, they may have to 'go through the motions' by deferring them until after the meeting.

General issues

If you are not satisfied with the way power is being exercised by your protagonist, you need nevertheless to consider the implications before you play the 'I want to speak to the manager' card.

Junior staff in commercial organisations are often constrained by procedure from making concessions which will give too much away, while more senior staff, with an eye to a broader agenda, may be able to make them. In a clothes shop the young man on the till may not be able to give you a discount on a jacket with a thread pulled, but the store manager probably can.

In a public service organisation giving concessions which junior staff have refused to make may be of no direct benefit to a senior member of staff. If the concession is challenged at still more senior level it will actually increase his risk. However, complaints about the *way* someone has done their job may have a considerable impact. If the official was rude, pompous or officious, or failed to keep you informed your complaint may well get a result. It is quite unlikely that the result will overturn the substantive decision however. Be clear what you want to achieve before you take this line.

Bureaucratic time-scales

There are three factors which determine the time-scale within which decisions are reached:

- the importance of the decision: the greater it is, the longer the time-scale involved;
- the size of the organisation: the larger it is the longer the time-scale;
- the degree of innovation: the more innovative the concept, the longer the time-scale.

In negotiations between representatives of a large organisation and representatives of a small one time-scales can provide a source of conflict. On the one hand small enterprises can often respond very quickly and flexibly because they do not have to negotiate decisions with a large internal constituency. On the other hand they may operate on small margins and tight time-scales. Typically the exact opposite is true for large organisations. The small enterprise needs to respond quickly or go out of business; the bureaucracy of the larger organisation needs time to achieve internal consent to and ownership of commitments.

However, there are circumstances in which these time-scale differentials can be used to advantage, collaboratively by both sides or manipulatively by one. The short response time of the small organisation can sometimes be used by a large one to get something done quickly which would be impossible within the large organisation itself. The bureaucratic time-scale can sometimes be of great advantage to the small agency too. Large bureaucracies do move slowly once they are off the track of a routine process. Once agreement in principle is reached, however, they seldom press for rapid implementation. And the negotiation itself can continue for many months provided some movement takes place. If the small agency is 'paying' rather than receiving, or the actions of the large agency necessitate expenditure elsewhere, the normal cashflow problems of small organisations trading with large ones are effectively switched.

The large agency will sometimes exploit the situation in reverse, as it may be in the position of a near monopoly purchaser. The negotiator knows that his small agency protagonist cannot afford to hold out for a better deal and uses that as an effective lever to obtain the result he wants.

The financial agenda

The financial agenda of your protagonist and her organisation will be constrained by one or more of the following three considerations:

- profit and loss,
- budget,
- procedure.

Profit and loss

This is the major financial constraint on any commercial agency under any circumstances, whatever the transaction. Profit and loss is incredibly straightforward but frequently misunderstood by the non-commercial world. No commercial organisation can do anything which it does not judge to improve or at least sustain its long-term profitability. Full stop. Every non-commercial negotiator should learn the previous sentence by heart! Commercial enterprises can be persuaded to reconsider their budgetary and procedural constraints, if they exist; but their long-term profitability is sacrosanct. This is not to say that profit is the only consideration for the commercial sector, but it is always the primary *financial* consideration.

Budget and procedure

In contrast, and equally misunderstood by the commercial sector, the public and voluntary sectors do not make profits or losses; they underspend or overspend a budget. In the non-commercial world efficient performance is much more difficult to measure. Two measures which do carry a lot of weight are the effective delivery of policy and procedure, and working within budget. In neither case does working more efficiently *per se* (i.e. the same for less or more for the same) carry much weight in reality. (Every public organisation goes through the motions of efficiency but, by comparison with budget and procedure, the sanctions are, in practice, very weak.)

It is usually obvious in context whether budget or procedure is the primary consideration. Consider the difference between 'We must have a report on the recent outbreak of salmonella poisoning within two months' and 'We have

£10,000 to spend before the end of the financial year to update our communication technology.'

If the primary consideration is budgetary you need to try to understand its likely impact: cost is usually an important consideration. But at the end of the year the real agenda might be to avoid an underspend. Under those circumstances the most useful question is often 'How much do you want to spend?'

Occasionally in the field of health and social services the agency is put in the impossible position of having to decide on procedure *and* budget where the two are irreconcilable. The covert rationing of services is an increasingly frequent example of this. The same process occurs in the social services. On 11 November 1997, the Department of Health issued a circular (LASSL (97) 13) 'clarifying' two recent judicial reviews. The 'Gloucestershire Judgment' and the 'Sefton Judgment' were both concerned with balancing procedure (in this case the assessment of individual need) with budget (availability of resources). The law and, to some extent, guidance seem to be saying that the care plan must be based solely on assessment of need. The appeal court seems to be saying that the assessment can be made with reference to the resources available, though of course, without explaining how. It is a particularly stark illustration of a dilemma that occurs with increasing frequency.

External factors

This is about understanding the political context in which you are negotiating. We have already seen, in the section 'Who is watching?' (pages 32–3), that it is sometimes an external factor which brings people to the table in the first place, and some may want to be there more than others. There are many factors which influence the relative position of the protagonists. In a trading relationship everyone knows about the classic buyers market/sellers market in which availability influences price, but there are many other influences. One of the examples in the following section is of negotiation between a greengrocer and a food hygiene inspector. If the negotiation had taken place in the aftermath of a major outbreak of food poisoning traced to a local greengrocer's shop, the whip hand would be firmly with the inspector. On the other hand, a local scandal about high-handed officiousness and over-zealous application of food hygiene regulations will reverse the situation completely.

As you prepare for a negotiation try to keep in mind the probable influence of the six major contextual factors.

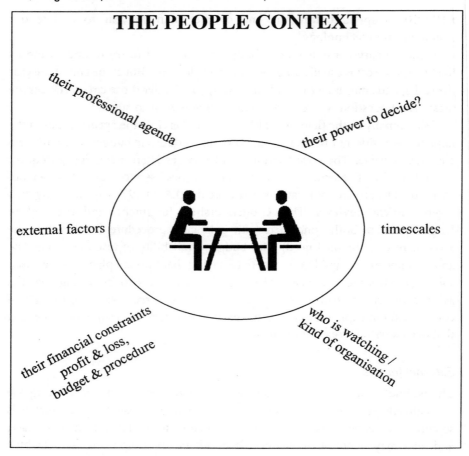

Figure 3.1

An extended illustration

It is quite difficult to give meaningful illustrations of single contextual influences, simply because contextual influences do not come singly! Instead, I have tried to illustrate a number of the factors I discussed in the previous section in this sequence of interlocking transactions (the first of which is not really a negotiation (Figure 3.1)). As you read through it try to relate the illustration to the factors.

The groceries

One of the most basic forms of human transaction is the purchase of small quantities of staples like food. In some settings, like a supermarket, it involves virtually no negotiation at all. In smaller shops and market stalls it often involves a little. Even when negotiation is involved in this kind of transaction it is not, at least in Britain and the United States, much about price. The routine haggling over price which is a trading characteristic of, for example, the Arab world is very unusual here. Americans will make endless demands about precisely what they want but not usually about what they will pay. The British typically accept what they are given at the price which is demanded!

Imagine you are buying your domestic supplies for a week or two, including onions. For some people 'value for money' is almost a religious mission but, for the sake of this story, you are not one of them. You want some nice, mild onions for salad and for cooking. You don't want to pay wildly over the odds for them, or indeed for any of your other vegetables, but a few pence either way will not break the bank.

You certainly do not want to go from the supermarket to the greengrocer and back to the supermarket. You don't want to spend the whole of your precious Saturday comparing prices, buying onions here, carrots there and apples somewhere else. You could of course go to a fruit and vegetable market and shop at different stalls in the same area. In such places prices are usually lower than elsewhere, because of low overheads and stiff competition, and quality is usually very good. But let us assume that there is not such a place within easy access of your home, or that you don't like going there.

1. You want onions.

2. They must be good quality.

3. They should be reasonably priced but, for low-priced things like onions, even a 25 per cent variation is within your acceptable range.

4. It should be possible to buy them together with the rest of your week's vegetables without shopping round too much.

This is not negotiation *per se*. There is usually none whatsoever in the supermarket and, even in the greengrocer's, goods are marked up at a 'take it or leave it' price. But some of the basic elements of negotiation are present. You want something which they have and the list above is of the conditions under which you are prepared to take them. (Different individuals would express the list differently according to their priorities: 'should' and 'must' in particular may not be in the same places I have put them.) If you cannot meet your most important criteria you may decide to forego onions altogether this week and use something else until they are met.

That is the most basic transaction. Someone wants something which is a small component of their total expenditure. There is no one else to consult. The conditions to satisfy in this case are at an absolute minimum.

Probably because life is too short we do not analyse our motives for this level of behaviour a great deal. Yet perhaps we should. The 'value for money' people get real pleasure from shopping around but very often they do not realise the potential which negotiation offers them for pursuing their hobby. They will plough endlessly through promotional material for special offers but seldom think in terms of saying 'I want what you offer but I won't pay the price you ask'. That is because they are not looking at what motivates the seller, only at what motivates them.

The greengrocer

In comparison to the shopper, the small self-employed shopkeeper operates at a much greater level of complexity. He has no-one to account to but himself but, unlike the shopper, he is both buying and selling. All the factors which are relevant to you are still relevant to him. In addition:

1. He wants you to buy his onions.

2. He must sell produce of a good quality. He takes pride in his business and in maintaining standards. He wants you to come back next week as well.

3. The onions should be reasonably priced. He will have some idea about the price-range you find acceptable but he doesn't want a reputation for selling over the odds for the same reason as before. You may pay the extra 25 per cent this week, but you may not be back again.

4. He would like you to buy the whole of your week's supply of vegetables from him.

When the greengrocer is selling to you, the shopper, the factors are simply the obverse of yours. When he is buying from the wholesaler, although the four factors are the same, they take on quite a different significance. The fundamental difference is that the buying is done with the selling in mind. Turnover, profit margin and continuity are the sources of business survival or success. In other words, although the factors determining his purchase are exactly the same as yours when you buy from him, his interpretation of the factors is entirely different. And the transaction between greengrocer and wholesaler will be very much a negotiation about price, quality, delivery and continuity.

The greengrocer will have little problem in understanding the motivation of his customers. We are all end-purchasers, so he simply has to think of why people want to buy fruit and vegetables. Big companies, of course, spend large sums on market research to gain a more detailed understanding of what makes people as purchasers tick. The basic motivation, certainly as regards something as fundamental as buying a staple food, is quite clear to all of us.

It is not hard for the greengrocer to understand the wholesaler either. His motivation is very similar to that of the retailer, the greengrocer. Wholesalers are almost always organisations, though often quite small ones, so the seller has his own constituency to consider. Both the seller and his constituency are concerned about the same things as the retailer. In this situation, whatever other complications there may be, understanding the context is seldom one of them.

Our greengrocer is a multi-faceted human being of course but, even as a greengrocer, the direct trading relationship is by no means the only one he must consider. He will have a relationship with the account manager at his local bank, which may be very straightforward or very fraught. He will purchase a range of goods and services to further his business. He has a relationship with the tax office, perhaps with the local TEC, perhaps with the Jobcentre. And he will have several links with the local authority connected with rates, environmental health, perhaps economic and business development. If he assumes the same interests which drive him and his wholesaler necessarily drive all these other people, he is in for a difficult time.

The bank

The greengrocer needs a loan. The environmental health inspector has just produced a report which requires, in effect, a complete refurbishment of the shop; so he needs several thousand pounds-worth of capital to finance it. The bank is a business like his shop but, using just that analogy, he will only understand the account manager's motivation to a very limited degree.

The account manager's motives in deciding whether to give him a loan will be governed by most of the contextual factors we discussed at the beginning of the chapter. She has no 'professional' agenda in the sense I have used the word earlier. But she is accountable to her branch manager. She has a certain level of discretion about the decision she makes. She is constrained by the time-scales which operate in the bank. Her financial agenda is decided on procedure. Finally, her decision is affected by external factors, which increase or reduce the likelihood of a loan and largely determine the rate of interest which will be paid.

If the greengrocer assumes that her problems are no different from his, he will be, at the very least, at a disadvantage.

The immediate constituency

The branch manager will need to be sure that the bank's finances are completely safe and that any offer which is made is within the policy, rate of interest and cash limits which pertain at the time.

The power to decide and timescale factors

Banks usually have explicit levels of discretion. It is perfectly legitimate to ask the account manager whether she can make a decision up to the level of the loan the greengrocer needs and she will almost always explain the position.

If she can lend up to £15,000 and he wants to borrow £12,500, clearly she is in a position to grant the loan; although she still needs to meet the criteria for lending. But if he wants to borrow £20,000 it is very difficult for him to discover what happens to process the decision. Does it go through 'on the nod' or does she undergo a grilling to convince someone else? Of one thing he can be sure: the higher the authority required to take the decision he wants, the longer it will take. If he is in a hurry he may decide to settle for less money but more quickly.

The account manager may also have limited discretion to take account of additional factors, but they too will be described in some detail in the bank's procedure. The greengrocer will do well to discover from her what these policy constraints are and to argue his case *in those terms.*

The financial agenda

The greengrocer may feel inclined to argue that the bank will make a fat profit from lending him the money (and you can be sure he will be right!). But he is missing the point. The bank is driven, in its small day-to-day decisions, entirely on procedure. The procedures themselves will be designed to maximise profitability and minimise risk, but – at least at the level at which our greengrocer is operating – they are not negotiable. The account manager must satisfy procedural criteria: if they fail to deliver the profit as predicted, she will not be held to account for that. She may, if her other criteria are met, be swayed by the knowledge that the borrower could be inclined to go to another bank for a better deal. In reality she is not likely to be in a position to improve her offer very much to retain him. Such matters as rates of interest and level of discretion are decided at levels of seniority far above her head.

External factors

Banks are very large organisations, so many other transactions within the organisation – and sometimes completely outside the management structure within which the local account manager operates – may impinge on the negotiation over the greengrocer's loan. The Bank of England is outside the control of the bank completely. It imposes base rates for borrowing and, sometimes, limits on lending, which will always be major factors in the negotiation. Neither of our protagonists can do anything about these things of course, but it helps to be clear about what is negotiable.

Turn the question round

In preparing his ground our greengrocer should ask himself 'What will she want from me?' Banks want to lend money. It is what they exist to do. He doesn't need to convince the bank that they should lend money. He needs to convince them that he is fit to borrow it. All things being equal, the account manager will be quite anxious that the greengrocer should help her to satisfy her criteria (and her managers) so that she can lend him the money. She has every reason therefore to make them as clear as she can.

It has been cynically said that banks only want to lend money to people who don't need it. Therein lies a profound negotiating truth. *You are never negotiating with anyone to convince them of what you want, only that you have what they want.* In this case the bank is looking for a safe place to deposit its money!

The local authority

As a food shop our greengrocer's premises are subject to inspection by an environmental health officer from the local authority to see that he is complying with the food hygiene regulations. The inspector wants him to make some changes to his premises which, he says, constitute a breach of the regulations as they are. Even the most tightly-drawn regulations are open to some interpretation round the margins and he has arranged to see the inspector to discuss just what is necessary. His agenda is to keep the cost and disruption of any changes he has to make to a minimum. At the same time he wants to avoid the slightest whiff of a suggestion of enforced closure or a reputation for being 'a dirty shop'.

Many small business people regard junior public service bureaucrats with ill-disguised contempt and contrast them unfavourably with the macho, risk-taking, wealth-creating entrepreneurs of the business community. If our greengrocer harbours such feelings, and wishes to make the pursuit of his agenda as difficult, painful and costly as the case will permit, he should give them full vent at the earliest opportunity! On the contrary, if he wishes to succeed he must treat his protagonist as an equal and with personal and professional respect. 'You are doing a necessary and important job. How can I help you to make sure that it is done properly (while at the same time keeping my own costs to a necessary minimum)?'

The food hygiene inspector has a 'professional' agenda. Like most people he is accountable to someone else. He makes practice decisions; even if they are formal recommendations to the authority they will be very powerful. He has a long time-scale: getting it right is far more important to him than getting it quick. Finally, his financial agenda is entirely procedural: the greengrocer cannot wait him out until his budget is exhausted!

The inspector works within a hierarchy so our greengrocer would do well to think about who and what this is. The senior officers will almost certainly have the same sort of professional agenda as the inspector himself. And, although he works in a democratically-controlled local authority, the elected members are unlikely to see much mileage in trying to push him towards a particular decision.

One of the key functions of the Environmental Health Department is to apply the food hygiene regulations which are designed to protect the public. Giving something away in this case is of no direct benefit to its officers; it actually increases their risk. If there is an outbreak of food poisoning in the area they will not be criticised for being over-cautious! So every step up the hierarchy makes the case more formalised and less open to negotiation. It increases the potential for conflict, which our greengrocer should do his utmost to avoid.

The local authority will be very conscious of the need to avoid complaints about the *way* the inspector has done his job. But it is important to remember that, although his seniors might censure the process by which he reached the conclusion, it does not mean that the conclusion itself will be changed. It is unlikely in the extreme that a council would overturn a professional decision which has been supported within its own professional hierarchy.

Summary

We could go on to explore the other contexts in which the food hygiene inspector moves, but I am sure that you have got the point already. You are probably not a greengrocer or a food hygiene inspector or a bank manager but these people, and others who work in quite different contexts, may be important to you. Effective negotiation often depends on careful preparation. Understanding your protagonist's starting points, the context in which he is working, will strengthen your position enormously. Even if some of your assumptions turn out to be wrong in the event, preparing to understand them will enable you to respond to the unexpected more flexibly.

Key learning points

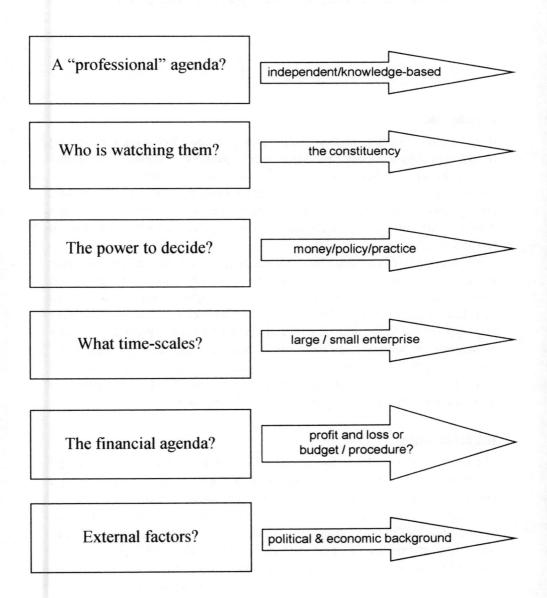

Figure 3.2

4. The Context: Organisations

Introduction

It is possible to accommodate your protagonists without betraying the slightest recognition of their personal, professional or organisational needs. At the level of complexity and sophistication demanded by the health and social services this is, to say the least, unlikely. In the previous chapter we tended to concentrate on your protagonists' needs as people. In this chapter we consider the imperatives which drive the different kinds of organisations which contribute to health and social services.

Of course there is no sharp line between people and organisations. The latter are merely organised collections of the former. The three kinds of organisation which are directly relevant to our discussion are the public sector, the commercial or private sector and the voluntary or charitable sector. Although they often employ very similar groups of staff and use very similar service delivery and management techniques, they are driven by fundamentally different imperatives. It is of the greatest importance, in any negotiations which take place between them, that these differences are understood on both sides. A lack of understanding is often the source of unnecessary conflict and confusion.

The public sector

The function of a public sector agency is to meet the policy commitments and priorities of itself and its parent authority, if there is one. The policies and priorities are ultimately always politically determined. If that function can be achieved and amply demonstrated everything else is secondary. Budgetary constraints are always secondary if the priority is compelling enough. The money is simply taken from another pot. So all you have to do to get what you want from your public sector protagonist is to demonstrate to her that in agreeing to your proposal she will meet the very first priority of her organisation. In order to achieve this simple (!!!) objective you need to respond to the policy of the organisation. That will be expressed in three ways: its values and aspirations, its priorities, and its language. And you must accord with all three.

Values and aspirations

Look at the policy statement of the public agency you are dealing with and especially at its aspirations. There are four value statements which are always there.

- Consultation with the public/patients/clients/consumers;
- Value for money (expressed in various ways);
- Increased efficiency;
- Working in collaboration with other agencies.

These might almost be regarded as the mantras of the modern public service, to be chanted repeatedly and, by themselves at least, to have little meaning. Let's look at each of them a little more closely.

Consultation with the public/patients/clients/consumers

Every public agency wants to do this, or at least to be seen to be doing it: none more so than health and social services. As an idea it is very valuable but it has to be in an area in which the public, etc., can express an informed opinion to have any practical meaning. A GP would not feel inclined to consult his patients about the kind of information system he installs, but he might well want to consult them about the kind of appointment system he runs.

Consultation is also something of a minefield. It is notoriously difficult to achieve meaningful consultation without laying oneself open to the twin charges of selectivism and tokenism. Selectivism is the process of choosing to consult only the consumers who will agree with you. Tokenism is installing one or two consumers, usually in a position of considerable disadvantage like in a board meeting, and calling it consultation. It is also potentially very threatening. If you start asking people open-ended questions about the service you provide they might:

(a) tell you that what you provide already is not very good, or

(b) tell you to change your operation in ways you don't want to hear.

Value for money

This can be bent to mean almost anything you want in order to meet the political priority of the moment. It is difficult to check in any context. In the health and social services, in spite of the fact that it provides a number of health economists with a very good living, it is virtually impossible.

Consider the heated debate about the NHS in the run-up to the 1997 election. The Labour Party said they would reduce the number of bureaucrats to provide more money for front-line services. The Conservatives argued that the bureaucracy was necessary to provide an efficiently run service. It was not a debate about what the health service should do, nor about how much it should cost, nor even about where the costs should fall. These are the real issues of political controversy. Instead the debate was about how to run it efficiently; how to get best value for money. At this level of generalisation it was completely meaningless. You can evaluate what you need to spend on the administration of this or that component of a service to deliver it effectively and cheaply. Anything more general than that really is nonsensical.

Increased efficiency

This is the other side of the value-for-money coin and it suffers from the same opacity arising from generalisation. It also confronts the negotiator with severe presentational problems as a feature of his case. Almost everyone starts from the assumption that they are already as efficient as they possibly can be. So, 'We can increase your efficiency' might fall on stony ground unless you can remove the implied sub-text 'because you are incompetent'.

You might strengthen your case by demonstrating that the outsider sometimes sees things which the insider does not, and that outside support for a change sometimes adds political weight. However, in most circumstances 'increased efficiency' is a value statement but not a priority in practice.

Working in collaboration with other agencies

This is a venerable public service aspiration which has always been, and remains, meaningless in itself. 'Working in collaboration' must relate to an objective to have any meaning. And, for it to happen in reality, the objective *as they see it* must be high on the priority list of each agency involved. This aspiration will often get you into conference with your public service protagonist (which is often very useful in itself) but don't rely on it as a bargaining chip. The obligation extends to meeting you; not to doing anything.

Other value statements

There are other values of great importance to health and social services agencies in the public sector, and very often voluntary and commercial agencies too. The most important of these are equal opportunities, race awareness, language policy, health and safety at work and quality assurance. The degree of emphasis with which each issue is treated may vary from agency to agency and from one part of the country to another. You and your own agency need to have a clear position and policy on each of them. Apart from their intrinsic importance your credibility will be severely eroded if it becomes apparent that you have not thought them through. Even if what you are offering your protagonist looks very close to their priorities, they will be less inclined to do business with you if your thinking on these matters is less well-developed than theirs. If it is in advance of theirs you may be able to offer them some added value. But be careful to avoid being patronising.

Priorities

In what way does the change you want them to make (buying your service; working more closely with you; not doing something which makes your life difficult) help to meet their priorities? First you need to know what they are. The best way to find out is to ask them. They will almost always be pleased to tell you; sometimes in far more detail than you need! You must find a way of fitting what you need from them with what they need from you to meet those priorities. Until you do so, you should postpone your meeting as an efficiency measure, and go back to preparing your ground.

Language

We will look at the different meanings of some keywords which are specific to the health and social services fields in Part II (in Chapter 9 in particular). The present section is about more general language issues. Politics and policies tend to be expressed in priority keywords. These keywords are often similar to the policy 'soundbite' concept, but they serve a different purpose. A single word or phrase is the carriage for a whole range of policy ideas and summarises them, sometimes for people who don't actually understand the nuances of the issue at all. Use the right keyword and the secretary will recognise that this is something important for whom X is responsible. Say exactly the same thing using different words and he will not recognise the significance and importance of your message. If you handle the issue sensitively your protagonist will often give you the right words to use. It is an issue of symbol rather than substance but no less important for that. It is easier to illustrate than to describe.

> When I was in the Social Services Inspectorate I was approached by some members of a voluntary organisation. They wanted funding to set up a community support team on an extremely depressed estate. I knew the work of this organisation and, from what its members had shown me, it was clear that they had prepared their ground well with the community and the enterprise would succeed given the chance. I also knew that 'community development' was a very low priority for finance at that time and, if the organisation bid for the programme under that title and using that language, the bid would fail.
>
> I suggested to the members of the organisation instead that they used 'crime prevention' as part of the title. It could also be included high on the list of the stated objectives, which it was anyway in different words, without changing the substance of what they proposed to do in any way. Their principal negotiator however felt that this would be some sort of affront to their integrity and would compromise their position. They

submitted the original proposal without the change. I added a note saying that it was really a crime prevention initiative under another name. Of course it failed just the same – as I knew it would.

When you ask about their priorities, as I suggested in the last section, listen carefully not only to what they say but how they say it; the words which they use. They will tell you in the language which is currently in vogue for them. Use that language. As far as you can use their words. In the previous example, if you were trying to sell the idea to the Home Office you would be using phrases like 'tough on the causes of crime'. If you were talking to the Department of Health you might achieve a happier result with 'an attack on poverty and deprivation'.

Notice something else about this. The two phrases in the previous paragraph contain aggressive, thrusting words, 'tough' and 'attack'. If your protagonist uses terms like that, pick up on them. If the language used is supportive, caring, 'touchy-feely', play that back instead, while if it is hard-nosed 'value for money' play on that. In other words, your main theme should be the component your protagonist is most interested in, expressed in the words he would use to describe it. I am not suggesting that you modify your objectives in doing this, although you may decide to do that for other reasons. Even less do I think you should compromise your principles. But you must present those aspects of your case which are of most interest to them, in language they want to hear. Those aspects may or may not be part of your main objective, but you have to convince them that, if they play ball, it will satisfy some of theirs.

It really is not an issue of integrity nor of being 'economical with the truth'. Consider the following example:

Bob runs an old people's complex providing residential and nursing care. It is crucial to his continuing viability that the local social services department continues to use his establishments and pays the premium he needs to provide a high quality of care and to make a profit. Bob knows his protagonists. He knows that the assistant director who makes the final decision has very high professional standards. But he relies entirely on the finance director to advise him about financial matters and on the advice of the community medical officer on all matters to do with nursing standards and medical care. So he talks informally, and separately, to the three of them.

1. With the assistant director he talks about the quality of life of the residents; their participation in decisions that affect them; the

regularity and thoroughness of professional review and the flexibility and warmth of the staff.

2. With the finance director he talks about value for money; rigorous financial management; the constant quest for greater cost-effectiveness.

3. With the medical officer he talks about the quality of nursing; staff qualification and training; rigorous hygiene procedures; state of the art equipment; access to medical support.

Deceitful? Not in the least. All those things are true about his establishment. In each conversation he talks about the issues of interest to the particular protagonist and uses the language each of them is comfortable with. His intention is to demonstrate to each of them just what a splendid establishment he runs judged by their own special standards.

One final point about language: don't be too ready to lead off with the substance of your purpose in the negotiation. Find out what your protagonists want by asking questions and listening to how they phrase the answers. You will get some useful ideas about how to lay out your own stall. Don't be afraid that they will think you are parodying them. It never occurs to most of us when we hear someone playing our music that there may be something more going on than a straightforward acknowledgement of its beauty, depth and elegance. Of course the more you know about their music in advance, the better you can rehearse your own.

And finally…

You need to recognise that public organisations are in a constant state of change. Because they are large organisations their statements of policy are always far ahead of the realities on the ground. Like all of us, what they say and what they do are often at odds.

You can make use of that in negotiation but be very careful how you do it. If you find a dissonance between what they say and what actually happens you may be tempted to 'rub their noses in it'. Control yourself! It will almost certainly backfire to your disadvantage. On the other hand if you can demonstrate that you can facilitate an improvement in their realities, bringing them closer to their rhetoric, you may be able to make them a very good offer.

The commercial sector

The most important thing to understand about the commercial sector is that its primary purpose is to make money. That is not a political statement but a factual observation. There is a huge gulf of understanding about this simple fact and it is obfuscated by other quite unrelated issues. Politicians of left and right, whether uncomprehendingly or cynically, have turned the fact into a statement of value and loaded it to their own ends. 'People not profits' and 'the wealth creators' are equally meaningless soundbites. The idea that a commercial organisation should or could work without profit is arrant nonsense. Then again so is the idea that only the commercial sector contributes to the wealth of the nation.

The first step towards understanding the commercial sector is to recognise that, as individuals, we are all 'commercial units'. The first reason why we work is to make money. It doesn't mean that paid employment is the only thing we do. It doesn't mean that the only value we get from work is money. It doesn't mean that we will do anything for money or that we are only interested in money, even in our paid work. But the first reason we go to work at all, for almost all of us, is to earn money. The public servant who is above such things, who sneers at 'grubby commercialism', is simply kidding himself and would do well to consider his own motives.

There are however major differences in what we are paid for and how we are paid. As a public servant you are paid to enact the public will, as interpreted by your council, or your board, or your ministers. As a professional you are paid to exercise your skilled judgement in doing so. You have an ethical obligation to the people who receive your service to report honestly, even if inconveniently, on what your professional knowledge leads you to conclude. But this is sometimes dimly understood by others.

A commercially-based professional is paid to do what his client wants and he won't be paid at all unless he does that. His professional strictures are exactly the same as those of his colleague in the public sector. Because he is paid by the client, it is not unknown for the commercially-based professional to downplay those aspects of his advice that are less palatable to the client. That is a matter of integrity and judgement. But not 'rocking the boat' is a strategy by no means confined to the commercial sector. Difficult decisions involving integrity and judgement are just as taxing for public servants.

The biggest difference is in how we are paid. People receiving a salary are paid a single block of money, spread through the year, to do everything they are paid to do. Commercial organisations are paid for individual projects or units of some kind. This leads to huge misunderstandings mostly, it must be said, on the part of salaried staff.

Some years ago I was responsible, as a public service professional, for child protection policy. A frequent complaint from other professionals was that general practitioners would not come to case conferences, much less to planning and development meetings and training events. The clear implication was that GPs were greedy and overpaid and would only do things for profit. Among the most vociferous complainants were some hospital consultants most of whom must have been paid more than GPs.

We (because I didn't understand this at the time either) misunderstood the issue. We were all paid a salary. For us, attending conferences and other meetings was a matter of priorities. We were paid to sort out these priorities and to do what seemed most important to discharge our responsibility. Low priorities dropped off the end but our salary stayed the same. GPs were (and are) independent contractors. They were paid a fee, based on number of patients, to provide them with a service according to a contract. Attending conferences was not part of that contract. For them it was not an issue of priority: they still had to provide the service for which they were contracted whether they attended the conference or not. To strip the issue to its essentials, we were being paid to attend case conferences but we criticised GPs for not doing it voluntarily.

The lesson from this is that if you want something from the commercial sector you must expect to pay for it. If you want to 'pick the brains' of a consultant with a particular expertise you should not be affronted when she sends you an invoice. That is how she earns her living. Unlike you she does not receive a BACS transfer to her account at the end of every month!

The voluntary sector

Public servants usually know what they want from the commercial sector but don't always recognise the need to pay for it. Their attitude to the voluntary sector is sometimes the antithesis of that. They expect to say exactly what they want and receive it, in exchange for smaller payment than they would have to make to the commercial sector. Voluntary agencies are, after all, charities with their own money to contribute!

In recent years there has been a lot of confusion about the changing relationship between the voluntary sector and the public service. The confusion is on both sides but, at least in the short-term, it has a greater effect on the voluntary sector.

Voluntary services raise contributions for their cause. They also seek public finance to provide services. They can expect to contribute to any project they run in a direct ratio to the degree of autonomy they anticipate in deciding what it should do and how it should be done. The more closely a project accords with the mainstream of public sector policy, the more public money voluntary services can expect to receive to support it. The notion is illustrated in the following graph (Figure 4.1).

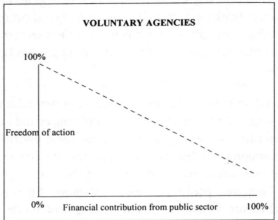

Figure 4.1

The voluntary sector is of course a group of charities – and charities are strange creatures. They are usually run by self-perpetuating oligarchies to pursue a mission statement which is often very broadly drawn. They are tightly controlled by the Charity Commissioners, one of the very first public regulatory bodies. In particular they may not pursue overtly political activity, an issue of much interpretative difficulty, and their members may not receive a financial reward nor benefit directly from the service which the charity provides. They are of course financed by voluntary contribution.

They are set up initially to provide or stimulate a service which the initiators think the state or the commercial sector either does not provide at all or provides inadequately. Almost by definition the newer, more radical charities are trying to push things up the public agenda and there is a delicate balance to be found between confrontation and collaboration. Push too hard and the public services just withdraw. Don't push hard enough and nothing changes; the objective is not achieved. The relationship with the public sector is, and probably should be, rather uneasy. The longer-established charities, of which there are many in the fields of health and social services, sometimes see themselves as having a more comfortable 'partnership' relationship with the public sector. As time goes on, public policy follows their early lead and eventually becomes very similar to theirs.

There is, however, a double confusion which has been highlighted in recent years by the development of the so called 'contract culture'. This has been partly imposed on local authorities by government action, as an extension of compulsory competitive tendering, and it has been partly adopted by them as a clearer way of working. (Their view; not necessarily mine.)

The confusion on the local authority side is that the relationship with the service-providing arm of the voluntary sector is now a straightforward commercial one. The local authority writes the specification and the agency delivers it (but more cheaply). The confusion on the voluntary side is that the service should be devised and delivered in partnership with the local authority, but should be paid for largely by the local authority.

Some of the most fraught and difficult negotiation courses I have ever run focused on that relationship as it was evolving. I think that this was mainly because it was not clear to anyone what either side actually wanted.

The use of the word 'partnership' is perhaps part of the problem because it implies a common starting point which seldom exists in practice. The following example illustrates the point.

A children's charity runs a residential establishment for children (an increasingly unusual service provided by children's charities, but one to which they may begin to return). One of their charitable aims is to provide services of a high standard and quality. For this group of young people the charity believes they need to provide fully qualified staff, psychiatric mentoring and external counselling. The local authority will not pay the premium needed to provide these services. It will only pay the cost per child per week, which it calculates is what it would pay to keep a child in the authority's own children's home, which does not have this infrastructure. Moreover, the authority will only pay for a child while he or she is actually occupying a place.

In other words, the local authority expects the charity to finance both the professional support infrastructure and any vacancies in the establishment, from voluntary resources. On the other hand, the authority values the service and would find it difficult to replicate if the charity was forced to withdraw it.

That is where the negotiation starts. Will the charity reduce its standards or pay from its own resources to provide them? Will the local authority provide better and more secure funding? Are there meeting points which can help both sides to achieve what they want?

The real obstacles to progress in a case such as this are the false perceptions on both sides. The local authority might think that the charity will provide precisely and only what it thinks is necessary as a way of 'getting the business'. But the charity's goal is to provide something which is good enough to have a long-term impact on children's lives. It would rather not run the service at all than provide mere containment. The charity might think that it can work out a 'partnership' with the local authority on the basis of a common objective. Because people are co-professionals sharing the same values, as they often are in this situation, it does not mean that they can ignore the very different objectives which their agencies exist to pursue. The fact that the protagonists are from the same professional stable can sometimes obscure the different organisational imperatives.

One final point: the key issues of basic values, priorities and language are often as important in the voluntary sector as in the public sector. When the negotiation is being conducted between them, a lively mutual recognition of the need to make those key issues compatible is helpful to say the least.

Key learning points

> The public sector is driven by political priorities
> rather than financial efficiency.
> You need to be aware of their underpinning values
> and to be clear where you stand on them.

> The language of public sector priorities is
> as important as the priorities themselves.
> You should use it when you negotiate with them.

> The primary purpose of the commercial sector is to make money,
> but it places no less value on standards and quality
> than the other two sectors.

> There are different implications in being paid by salary (i.e.. by time)
> and by fee (i.e.. by output).

> The public and voluntary sectors have their own agenda and priorities.
> They must both be willing to pay to see them included in the outcome.
> It is not a straightforward client/provider relationship between them.

Figure 4.2

5. Strategy and Tactics

Introduction

Up to now we have looked at a range of things which create the climate and context of negotiation. In this chapter we consider some of the knowledge and skills you will need to negotiate successfully. Most professionals in the health and social services fields already possess both, but they don't necessarily apply them very well.

> In war, as in politics and business, strategy tends to be the term used for a grand design or plan of action to be taken against an enemy, political opponents, or to ensure that a business enterprise is successful. Tactics, when there is a contrast with strategy, tends to be used of the detailed means adopted in carrying out such a grand design. (*Fowler's Modern English Usage,* Third Edition, p.745)

Long ago and far away we used to have endless semantic discussions about what was an aim, what was an objective, what was a strategic objective, what was an operational objective, what was a strategy, and what was a tactic. It is a pity that none of us thought to read Fowler then! It doesn't really help to spend too much time deciding if this or that plan of action is strategic or tactical. It will often depend on the context.

In general it is useful to consider the plan of action you prepare for the encounter as your 'strategy', and the way you manage the components of the encounter as the 'tactics'. There is of course no sharp line between the two and part of your strategy can be to prepare for your response to different contingencies.

> If they say that they cannot possibly offer more than £275 per bed per week, then we take the line 'If we accept that then will you discuss a premium over that basic figure for special needs?'

The two essentials are to prepare your ground well and to develop, or more often simply to deploy, your skills during the encounter.

Planning your campaign

Your purpose

The one thing that is definitely strategic rather than tactical is deciding what you are going for. You might tactically retreat but you must start with a clear objective. The very first thing you need to do to prepare for your negotiation is to be absolutely clear what its purpose is: *what do you want?* I make no apology for constantly repeating this. More negotiations fail because people are not clear what they want than for any other reason. If you think about it, it is actually impossible by definition to succeed unless you do know.

A GP group practice has had a frustrating time over many months with the social services children's team. The team makes unreasonable demands for information and attention. It is evasive and uninformative about what it is doing and about its plans for various children. Enough is enough; at the next practice meeting two of the partners are set up to meet the area officer and 'get it sorted out'.

They arrange a date and confirm by letter that they want to meet 'to sort out a number of difficulties that the practice has experienced with the social work team during the past several months'.

They have a list of grievances from their colleagues. The area officer also prepares a defensive brief in consultation with members of his team and a list of 'counter-claims'. Guess what happens at the meeting! It is sometimes called 'a Mexican stand-off'.

Why did the meeting fail? Both sides were preparing for a court case without a judge. They were preparing to win a competition, not to find a solution with which both could live more comfortably. If either had started their preparation by asking 'What do we want out of this?' they would have had more than a fighting chance of achieving something.

Sometimes the answer to the question is very straightforward. More often than not it has a number of interdependent parts and degrees of acceptability, as in the following illustration.

The acceptable minimum

> A charitable organisation wants to establish a family centre in a deprived community offering a range of services, and they want £300,000 a year to run it.

In this case the primary want is the family centre. The £300,000 forms part of the next question: *what is the minimum acceptable?* Assuming the £300,000 is the optimum figure they have in mind, there must be some lower figure that they can live with, if they have to, in order to achieve their primary aim. What is it? This is sometimes a very complex question, and it probably would be in this case. What if the authorities bore the capital cost? What if they seconded some staff? What if the ideal list of services was trimmed to reduce cost? When all those questions are settled, there must be a baseline position below which the charity cannot afford to fall, however much they want to see the family centre developed.

The minimum acceptable varies enormously according to the type of issue under negotiation. For the GPs in the first example (page 58) almost any improvement on the current situation would have been acceptable, provided they did not have to pay too high a price to gain it. The trouble was that they were not thinking in those terms.

Here it is useful to make some distinctions about the type of negotiation which is taking place. The generic description is an encounter between two or more parties from which each has some benefit to gain.

One key distinction we have already discussed. Is the negotiation a commercial transaction in which a direct exchange of benefits (usually money for goods or services, but not inevitably) is being contemplated? Or is it a non-commercial one where the benefits are indirect or are delivered to a third party?

Is the public sector ever engaged in 'commercial' transactions at all? It is certainly always dealing on behalf of third parties (i.e. the public). Consider the difference between a supermarket chain buying from food producers and a health trust buying from a computer company. If the supermarket buys the wrong goods at the wrong price it will lose market share which will eventually result in redundancies, possible takeover and even bankruptcy. If the trust buys the wrong computer system it results in poorer patient service and loss of money to the health service. The point is that, while the supermarket is always trading (and negotiating) for itself, the public service is always negotiating on behalf of its public. There will be protests about this from both sides. Some within the NHS will argue that the health trusts are negotiating for themselves within an internal market. The supermarkets will argue that they are buying to get the best deal for their customers. I leave you to decide. My purpose in making the distinction is to help you clarify your own and your protagonist's priority objectives.

A second distinction is between those encounters in which it is possible, *in extremis*, for the parties to walk away from the table empty-handed, and those in which it is not. However much the charity in the example on page 59 wants to establish its centre, if the authorities cannot, or will not, meet its minimum requirement it must, in the end, withdraw from the proposition altogether.

In the other example, the doctors and the social workers cannot simply walk away from each other. In that sense there is no bottom line: they both have to do the best they can however poor they perceive that to be. Their conditions of service and their professional responsibility to those they serve give them no choice. However minimally they may do it in practice, they simply *have* to work together.

What do they want?

Now you know what *you* want, and what is the least *you* are prepared to settle for, you can start thinking about *them*. Using all the indicators you have available, ask yourself 'What are these people in business for, and what does that imply about what they want from this encounter and what they simply must have?' Try to get inside their heads. They are not you and they don't work for your organisation. It is not enough to imagine what you would do if you were them: 'Well, this is what they jolly well ought to want!' You need to imagine what they will do because they are them.

The best way to find out is to ask them what they want and to keep asking them. Keep in touch with your protagonists: not just in the context of the immediate issue under discussion, but more generally too. Exchange ideas: engage them in regular discussion. You will understand them much better if you do. As we said right at the start, the more you know about them, the more likely it is that your negotiations will succeed.

You know what you want and you think you know what they want. From that you can work out the common ground and areas of possible conflict. How can you handle the conflicts? In Chapter 2 I introduced you to a planning matrix which many people find useful (Figure 2.1). Here it is again. Don't rush to the nuts and bolts of the process before you are as clear as you can be about the fundamentals. The negotiation will be a lot easier to handle from a firm foundation.

WHAT DO THEY WANT?	WHAT DO I WANT? **(a) Most desirable outcome** **(b) Minimum acceptable outcome**
THEIR STRENGTHS (What strengthens their case to get what they want from us)	**MY STRENGTHS** (What strengthens my case to get what I want from them)
THEIR WEAKNESSES (What weakens their case to get what they want from us)	**MY WEAKNESSES** (What weakens my case to get what I want from them)

Figure 5.1

Timing

Timing is both a strategic and a tactical issue with several aspects.

Timescale

Timescale is sometimes an important aspect of somebody's minimum requirement. 'I would like to have this centre up and running by September, but I must have it open before the end of the financial year (otherwise it will fail).'

The timescale for a result is often the biggest area of conflict in the health and social services fields. We will examine the timing and cashflow dissonance between local and health authorities in Part II, and I have already mentioned some of the timing conflicts between large public and small voluntary or private agencies. For the moment we just need to remember that they exist. I have known projects on which there has been complete accord about objectives, costs and operational details. They have failed, nevertheless, because one side was unable to make a final decision before the deadline for the other side had passed. Sometimes it does not occur to anybody that this is an issue at all until it is too late to do something about it.

The questions to think about are: 'When do we want a result? When do we think they will want a result? Can we find ways of meeting both needs?'

Timing the whole process

Simulation exercises are an excellent way of learning about negotiation, especially if they are fairly close to the kind of negotiation we actually do. But negotiation doesn't happen in a bottle, isolated from all that has gone before and will come after. You cannot simulate the whole process, only the preparation for and conduct of one meeting. In the real world, success is at least as much to do with setting up the negotiation as with the event itself. And timing is an important aspect of this.

Outside the small, day-to-day transactions, reaching a result (an agreement) inevitably involves several stages. The stages follow a definite sequence and there is a tendency to leap too swiftly towards the final stages before the earlier ones have been satisfied. The table below illustrates the process (Figure 5.2). The illustration relates it to the purchase of a large item like a car or a house. The four stages are of course very much simplified even for this comparatively straightforward negotiation. Sorting out the detail can be quite difficult and reaching agreement about price (and most importantly the basis on which the price is concluded) can be complex and time-consuming.

The issues in sequence	Protagonist A	Protagonist B
1. The issue in principle	I want to buy a car; you want to sell a car.	I want to sell a car; you want to buy a car.
2. The issue in detail	I want a small, new car	I think you want this one which I have for sale.
3. The areas of conflict	I want £3000 for my old car.	I can only give you £2500 against this one.
4. Resolving the conflict	I won't accept less than £2750 for my old car.	I can give you £2750 against this one with a higher mileage

Figure 5.2

Now let us consider this in the case of a non-commercial example which demonstrates negotiation as the outcome of a process rather than as a single event.

The team leader of a social services juvenile justice team has received repeated messages from her team that the big problem of the moment is school exclusions of 14–16-year-olds. These alienated and delinquent youngsters, with no school to go to, are getting into trouble during the day. And her staff are finding it very difficult to help them to relate to anything outside their own subculture because they have no external structure to their lives.

The team leader wants to have an impact on the schools but knows it is no use simply saying to them 'Please do not exclude children any more'. They are doing it for good reason, as they see it, and she must find something to offer in return before they will take any notice.

In the terms of Figure 5.1, she has not yet identified the whole issue in principle. She knows what she wants, but not what the schools want. So instead of opening a discussion directly about school exclusion she gets herself invited to a head teachers' meeting to talk about working more effectively together to prevent and manage youth crime. There the issue of school exclusion is raised and she discovers that the head teachers feel vulnerable and unsupported. Their staff do not know how to handle the minority of youngsters who behave in a seriously disruptive way in school and they have the choice of exclusion or serious and contagious disorder.

So, the team leader has discovered that what the head teachers want is support. She runs a team of people with considerable skill in communicating with seriously alienated youngsters. They also have the backup and advice of health service colleagues to enable them to unravel the causes of the more intractable and inexplicable behaviour. Now she has something to offer. 'If you stop excluding children then I will provide support to help you manage them.'

From that point she can begin to negotiate, first with one school then with others:

- first, the *principle* of providing support from her team;

- then, the *detail* of what that support might mean;

- then, the *areas of conflict:* the schools want a full-time presence; there is no possible way she can provide that; and

- finally, the *details of the agreement:* how much time will be provided, when the programme will start and how long it will run before it is reviewed.

Timing in meetings

In planning for meetings it is useful to try to anticipate how your protagonists might time their approach to the subject and what you can do to respond. How long is the meeting scheduled for? At what stage should you start moving gently from principle to detail and from detail to issues to be resolved?

The same general principles which apply to timing in general also apply to timing in meetings. You need to go in sequence through the issue in principle, the issue in detail, the possible sources of conflict to resolve and finally the resolution. If one of the protagonists jumps ahead and the other is not able to pull the discussion back on track the possibility of a good outcome is reduced.

It is important, however, not to be trapped by the time structure of the meeting. Unless you have no second chance it is better to break off when you have gone as far as you are comfortable with. Don't allow yourself to be bounced into a conclusion you do not want, simply because time is running out. You may need to consult your constituency about some of the new proposals which your protagonists have put on the table. You may need time to think and work through some of the financial and other complexities.

There is an age-old salesperson's ploy which goes 'If you sign up for these today I can make you a never-to-be-repeated offer of...discount'. It has many manifestations outside the buy and sell situation. A common committee-room gambit from the same stable is 'We have discussed this endlessly and we seem to be getting nowhere. Either we resolve this right now or we can just forget it'.

Avoid the temptation to use these bouncing ploys on others, and treat those which are used on you with great scepticism. The acid test is to ask yourself whether, if you refuse to accept the offer on the table today, you can still agree to accept it tomorrow if you decide to. The answer is usually yes.

That is not to say that timing issues do not affect what is on offer as we have already seen. It is usually clear from the context which kind of issue it is by the way the subject is approached. The bounce is usually accompanied by a brouhaha of threats or promises and demands for a decision *now* or *by close of play today*. The whole point is to make you jump without pausing to think. The genuine timing problem is usually accompanied by rational explanation and gives you sufficient thinking and consultation time. 'There is a committee meeting at the end of this month; I do need your response by then at the latest.'

Timing and money

One of the most difficult timing issues in our culture is the point at which money is introduced (where it is an issue in the negotiation). As a consultant I have experienced the question 'What do you charge?' in almost the opening line of a discussion. At the other end of the spectrum I have gone through a whole agreement without the subject being mentioned at all: I am left to charge whatever I please. I do not allow that situation to arise any more. My closing shot, if it has not come up before, is to say what my charges will be and seek their agreement. They of course are in a very weak position to disagree by that stage and I would prefer to leave the room with an agreement about which they are content, even if I receive a slightly lower reward as a result. I want to come back in the future so the last thing I want is for them to feel 'ripped off' but unable to do anything about it.

When should you introduce the subject of money? By stage three, (identifying the conflicts), both sides have outlined and detailed their requirements. They are both committed in principle to reaching agreement, and the issues to resolve are the conflicts. The subject of money is almost always an issue of conflict. The side contributing it wants to make the lowest acceptable offer. The side receiving it wants to make the highest acceptable offer. If both sides are committed to reaching an agreement they will do everything they can to find a way of meeting in the middle.

Tactics

High value to them; low cost to you

Always try to find things to offer which are of low cost to you but high value to them. And seek things from them which they can part with easily but which give you great benefit. These imbalances are always present. They stem from unequal distribution of expertise, technology or equipment; from different organisational structures and different accounting arrangements. They can make huge differences and sometimes turn a lose/lose situation into a win/win one.

A voluntary organisation wants to set up a day centre. The proposal has been around for some time and the local authority is keen to support it. Details are worked out and a tentative budget agreed. Suddenly the local authority is faced with an 8 per cent reduction in its total budget and the relevant department, social services, must bear its share.

The project seems bound to fail. The agreed budget was hard-negotiated and there is no way the voluntary organisation can possibly reduce its proposed expenditure by 8 per cent, or increase its own contribution any further. Part of the budget was to enable them to lease a building to convert into the centre. Instead, they manage to find a local authority building which they can use without charge and which the local authority will convert for them, also without charge. Best of all this capital work appears under a completely different budget head so the whole thing can be achieved with no apparent cost, at least to those accountable for the relevant budget. On the other hand the voluntary organisation has acquired the use of a facility of very high value to them. If there is a loser at all he or she is completely off the stage of play!

That example was made possible partly by avoiding the commercial property market and partly because of the organisational and accounting arrangements within the local authority. Now let us look at an example arising from unequal distribution of expertise, technology and equipment.

I am negotiating with a community health trust to provide most of its senior and supervisory staff with negotiation training in the form of a series of seminars. Part of the deal which I offer is a handbook for participants to use during the seminars and to refer to afterwards. If I design and write the handbook will they reproduce it with a bound and laminated cover? They are happy to do that. They have a laminator, a binder, and a high quality colour photocopier, and can produce the 250 copies we estimate may be needed quickly and cheaply. And in any case the cost of doing this does not show up on the training budget for this course. I have none of that equipment and I would need to get the work done externally at considerable cost. On the other hand I do have a copy of the handbook on the hard drive of my computer already. All it requires is an hour or two to make minor drafting amendments so that it is suitable for this new situation. The deal is of high value to me and low cost to them.

If...then

Don't give things away. When you put an offer on the table make it clear that you do so in return for something else. The best way to do this is always to precede such offers with 'if'.

Some years ago I was running a seminar on negotiation with Alan Coote, one of the people who has advised me on this book. The participants were a group of people from the independent residential and nursing care sector. The course contained a simulation exercise which was supposed to be an encounter with the local director of social services and his team. Its purpose was to negotiate the price, terms and conditions for residential and nursing care during the coming year. The 'care sector' team had decided to offer to accept a basic charging rate pegged at the previous year's charge. In return they wanted a range of special needs additions for residents requiring higher than normal levels of care.

The spokesperson opened this phase of the negotiation by saying 'We are happy to accept that the bed per week charge should remain at last year's level…' Before he reached the second sentence the 'director' said 'That is very helpful of you. I am sure that will make my case before the committee, who have been putting me under pressure to seek a cut, a great deal easier.'

It was a moment of pure poetry…and very rapid learning! The 'care sector' team did the sensible thing: they asked for an immediate adjournment.

Adjournment

It is very difficult to recover your sense of direction 'on the hoof' if matters take an unexpected turn. If your team suddenly starts to fall apart, if you start to lose your sense of direction, if you are increasingly uneasy about the way things are going, ask for an adjournment to consider the implications of the stage you have reached. If you try to plough on regardless in the hope of regaining your position you will probably end up in some chaos.

If you do this in a sensible and mature way, and, of course, not too often, you will not put yourself at any disadvantage. Always remember that you are trying to reach an agreement. You are not trying to win a competition.

Speaking, listening and pausing

You are trying to find a way to meet your protagonist's needs. You are not going to find out much about them while you are talking. The good negotiator develops the skill of active listening, a skill which health and social services professionals should be developing anyway for other purposes. You probably already have this skill which you apply to good effect as a professional and a manager. It is absolutely no different in this context.

Anxiety makes people inclined to talk more than they should. Listen to what your protagonist wants. Respond to it, without losing sight of what you want. If you can't think of an answer to a question addressed to you *don't waffle*. A thoughtful pause can be very powerful and assertive. The non-verbal message 'I'm thinking about what you have just said' is usually positively received, provided it is not accompanied by a sharp intake of breath!

Managing your team

Do you have any 'loose cannons' on your team? They can cause you a lot of trouble if you fail to manage them, preferably as part of your pre-planning. You have a number of options, though some may not be available in practice:

- get them off the negotiating team altogether;
- give them strict instructions to keep quiet, except on specific issues;

- give them a well-defined rôle;
- make it very clear in the meeting that they do not represent your collective view.

The well-defined rôle is the best option if you can manage it. The potential offenders could be given the task of making sure all the issues are covered, for example – in effect a responsibility to manage, or at least monitor, the agenda. If all goes well they will be too busy concentrating on their important task to engage in flights of fancy.

The departmental team met with certain charities to talk about their funding and to monitor progress. The charities received annual core funding for their headquarters costs because they were meeting needs deemed to be important to the realisation of government policy. Inevitably, of course, the funding was less than they would have liked. The actual amount was not decided during the meetings because a submission covering a number of charities had to be put to ministers. The department was usually able to give them a 'without prejudice' idea of what might and might not be funded. This enabled them to respond on the day and to do some planning with a rough indicative budget in mind.

One such charity group contained a notorious 'loose cannon'. At the first meeting she attended she launched into a diatribe against the incompetence of the departmental team – their lack of compassion, their lack of insight and their generally craven behaviour in not demanding more for her cause.

When this happened it threw the rest of her colleagues, of which there were too many for their own good, into disarray. They all started talking at once. Some were effectively apologising for the insult; some were trying to keep the substance of what she had said – 'it's not enough' – while trying to distance themselves from the tone and personal abuse. They completely lost their agenda and, in the end, their team leader asked if they could withdraw 'to do some more research' and return in a few weeks. The departmental team agreed.

They returned in about six weeks. The 'loose cannon' was still part of their team and she did exactly the same thing as before. This time the rest of the group remained completely silent. After a clearly-marked pause their leader picked up the thread of the discussion again as if nothing had happened. They had obviously decided that they could neither control her nor get rid of her, but they certainly managed her. It was extremely effective.

Managing unequal commitment; the reluctant protagonist

It sometimes feels as though the protagonist who occupies the venue and sets the agenda controls the show. Remember, however, that negotiations take place because both sides think something might be gained from them, or at least fear the consequences of refusing to meet.

The head of one professional group might be very reluctant to meet the head of another. He might regard it as a complete waste of time or be very threatened by the prospect. While he might go to considerable lengths to avoid it, he is most unlikely to refuse in the end. Many people are difficult, uncooperative and obstructive, but very few are willing to be seen in that way and even fewer are willing to face criticism for it.

Managing a meeting like that is very different from managing one in which there is equal interest in the outcome on both sides. It will probably be their venue but almost certainly your agenda.

You need to make sure that the agenda starts off with something which will interest them. It can be something they want for themselves or their organisation, but it is more likely to be something they wish to avoid, like embarrassment or criticism. Meetings which start from a mutual interest can be rescued from a poor beginning. Meetings which start with one side going through the motions cannot.

It follows that this kind of meeting requires very careful preparation on your part. If it is the prospect of a complaint that the other side fears, try to get signals to them, in one way or another, that you jolly well will make a complaint if you don't reach an outcome which you find minimally acceptable.

Nuclear threat

One way of tackling unequal commitment, especially when you think the protagonists are unlikely to approach your minimum requirement, is nuclear threat. I call it that because such outcomes – court action, industrial tribunal, surcharge, expulsion – are often as damaging to the side exercising the threat as to the side against which it is exercised. Don't use a nuclear threat you are not prepared to deliver in the final analysis. If you don't believe you will do it you can be sure they won't either!

I hope it doesn't require emphasis that this really is the last ditch, when all else fails and has failed consistently. When you do reach that point the problem is getting the other side to believe you have reached it. If you have spent months trying to accommodate them and looking for the middle ground, the sudden appearance of a cannon on the lawn is in danger of being interpreted as a tactic. So it shouldn't be sudden. Quiet messages should precede the event which say 'Look, this can't go on for ever. We don't want to bring in the artillery but if we have to the guns will be loaded and primed.'

The potential for collateral damage is considerable. Try to avoid pitching your minimum acceptable result above the level at which they consider it worth their while to risk discomfort rather than accede. Sometimes, however, the issue is too compelling for that.

A black female nurse was passed over for promotion by the trust. She was well qualified, highly respected and regarded as a good team player. There was strong circumstantial evidence that one senior member of staff had been largely responsible for vetoing her application. The union had quite a file on the actions of this man, in whom racism had been strongly suspected and sexism had been beyond doubt.

The union negotiator was pretty sure that he could get an admission from the trust that the nurse had been unfairly treated and the nearest thing to a guarantee that she would be promoted next time a suitable vacancy arose. However, the nurse wanted nothing less than the suspension of the offender. The local executive of the union, with an eye on the earlier offences against their members, backed her. The negotiator was almost sure that the trust would not go that far and that a bruising fight would ensue. Both the nurse and the executive decided that it was a price they were prepared to pay.

Money tactics

In my youth I used to be a farmer and sold cattle at auction. It was common practice to negotiate a one-to-one deal before the cow went into the auction ring and withdraw her by agreement. It was also common practice for the seller to give the buyer £5 or £10 back 'for luck' at the handshake. On more than one occasion I sold a cow to a wily old Yorkshire farmer for £5 more than I thought I would get at auction, only to give him £10 back 'for luck' as we shook hands!

Apparently fixed costs or prices can very often be massaged up or down without anyone losing face or breaking the rules by which they are constrained. 'We are only able to pay £200 per day.' But how long is that day? Are expenses added to that figure? Do they bear the cost of all materials and accommodation? 'Our budgetary ceiling is £115,000.' But can some of the additional costs be found from other budgets; can we find a contribution from the health authority/social services department/somewhere else?

In short, money appears to be far more immutable than it actually is. You can often negotiate around a fixed sum of money. Look for non-cash extras or savings. Find ways of adding or subtracting money in a way which does not appear to alter the fixed sum (like expenses). Define what the sum will buy more tightly or more generously. (How many hours in 'a day'; how many bottles in 'a case'?)

Dubious tactics

People who see negotiation as 'war by other means' make much of tactics which put the protagonist at a disadvantage. There are physical gambits like sitting with your back to a bright window or behind an imposing desk. There are power games which put one of the protagonists at a status disadvantage, like name-dropping or talking in professional jargon. There is aggression or distress, feigned or real, which exerts pressure to accede to a demand. In the next two chapters we look at how to handle this behaviour in others without losing a sense of purpose and direction.

Suffice it to say for now that such tactics are best avoided altogether on your part. Negotiation should be conducted in an honourable and ethical way and such games sit uncomfortably with that. In any case, though they may gain you short-term advantage, they will lose you long-term goodwill. As a negotiator you want to be seen as tough, but fair and open. A reputation for dirty tricks is something you can do without. And these tricks can easily backfire. You are giving your protagonist reasons to kick you if he can, sometimes even to his own disadvantage. That is definitely not a clever thing to do.

A middle manager in a voluntary agency tried to persuade a public service team to finance a project. He failed on this particular occasion because, as the team made clear, it did not meet current priorities. He went to the head of his agency, a national figure, told her a rather partial story and asked her to intervene with the director. The outcome resulted in considerable embarrassment for the head of the agency (who should have known better herself), no progress on the project and a loss of goodwill which caused considerable damage to the agency. The wise negotiator knows when to let go!

Key learning points

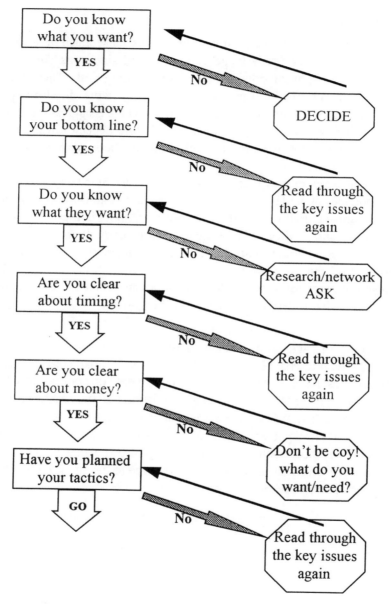

Figure 5.3

And finally, avoid dubious tactics: they will do you no good in the end!

6. Negotiation is People Talking

Introduction

Thus far we have concentrated on the purpose of negotiation and the context in which it takes place. The remaining two chapters of Part I are about managing the event itself: how you can influence the outcome you want by the way you behave, and how you should respond to your protagonist's behaviour. A small opportunity can be turned into a success by skilful handling. An agreement waiting to be made can be turned into a Mexican stand-off or open warfare by crass and incompetent behaviour. This chapter in particular is designed to help you to achieve the former and avoid the latter!

Signals

Written signals

A letter or a report has two potential aspects: substance and signals. Consider this example: a student asks his bank for a loan and receives one of the following replies:

1. I find it incredible that you should seek a further loan with your credit record and most emphatically refuse to allow you further credit etc.

2. Thank you for your letter. I regret to inform you that the bank is unable to accede to your request on this occasion. Please call at the bank if you would like to discuss the matter further.

3. I am sorry to tell you that I am unable to agree to your request at this point. However, if you will call at the bank to discuss your needs I am sure we will be able to find a solution to your current problems.

4. I was most concerned to receive your letter. It is vital that you now get your financial affairs in order. Please call and see me at your earliest convenience etc.

The first three replies all contain the same substantive message of refusal but they are very different because they contain different signals. The signal in the first letter can be roughly translated as 'over my dead body'. This kind of gratuitous verbal violence is much beloved of certain junior bank staff and other officials who are not destined to rise far above their present level. No good can possibly come of such finality and the embellishment of an implied insult only makes matters worse. If the decision is subsequently reversed at more senior level the bank appears inconsistent and the writer of the first letter appears foolish and impotent. If the student takes umbrage and moves his account elsewhere the bank might have lost fifty years' business to sustain someone's ego.

The second letter contains no signal of any description. It is simply a polite refusal. Even the phrase 'on this occasion' means nothing more than 'this has no implications for any future decisions'. The final sentence is also substantive only. It tells the student what to do next, but gives no indication of possible outcome.

The third letter contains a very clear signal and, in its way, proves the same kind of hostage to fortune as the first. The student gets the message 'don't worry; we'll get you out of this mess'. What if, in the event, it is not possible to broker an arrangement? I am not suggesting that signals in writing are to be avoided, but phrases as unequivocal as 'I am sure' which appear in print are usually unwise.

The fourth letter is different from the other three: it contains a signal but no substance except an invitation to negotiate.

Verbal signals

The spoken word shares with the written word the same two aspects of communication. Whereas signalling should be very restrained in written business communication, it is the very essence of face-to-face discussion. It is virtually impossible not to give signals during such encounters. If you have ever met officials who are quite determined not to give you anything more than the substance of a message (sometimes for very good reason on their part) you will know that it feels incredibly hostile! They might be trying to remain neutral, but the signal is almost always received as negative.

Most verbal signalling is an extension of the 'if...then' theme. They are telling you, or you are telling them, what needs to happen to move closer to agreement. The first rule of negotiation practice is *listen with care*. The second rule is *make sure they hear what you are saying.* Signals are very easy to misinterpret, especially if you only listen to the first part of them. Many verbal signals take the form 'no' – 'but' – 'thus'. 'No' is voiced. 'But' is sometimes voiced, sometimes silent. 'Thus' is usually silent; you must infer it for yourself. Here are a few examples (Table 6.1). Written down like this, of course, they are reasonably obvious but verbal exchanges are seldom so clear, concise, sequential and uninterrupted. You need to learn and hone the skill of listening and conveying clear signals by constant practice and by reviewing negotiations in which you have participated or observed.

Verbal Signals		
(message in italics implied rather than voiced)		
NO (explicit)	**BUT / AS** (often explicit)	**THUS** (usually implied)
I could not possibly agree to those conditions.	You have set them out in this protocol.	*If we are to make progress you will need to set them out differently.*
We seem to have reached an impasse; perhaps we should take a short break.	*I still think it is worth trying to find a solution.*	*See what you can come up with and so will we.*
I'm afraid my committee would never agree to pay that price.	*Everything else we have discussed except the price seems OK.*	*Can we find a different price structure?*
You have made no concessions to the current climate/cash limits etc.	*I have to demonstrate to my constituency that I have won some concessions from you.*	*Can you come up with something for me to present to them?*

Figure 6. 1

Many verbal signals which contain the 'no/but/thus' message do not come in that order nor do they fit neatly into the boxes. The message is implied nevertheless. 'I think we need to explore that issue in a little more detail' might mean a number of additional things in context, but it always means 'because it is not good enough for us as it stands'. Messages about the language used, the way financial elements are framed, or about priorities often mean 'You need to make changes in the way this is presented in order for me to be able to sell it to my constituency'.

You need to give clear signals to your protagonists and to guide them towards your 'thus' conclusions if they are missing the point. You sometimes need to help them out of holes of their own making. 'I could not agree to that under any circumstances' or 'I find it incredible that you should even consider proposing such a thing.' This is the kind of statement people with a burning desire to paint themselves into corners quite often make. They need help to escape with dignity. Sometimes the best way to do it is to allow them to restructure your proposal so that, even though it means the same thing, they can accept it in their terms without loss of face. Sometimes you may have to find a way for them to have 'misunderstood' your original proposal by rephrasing or elaborating it for them. They can then say 'Ah! I thought you were saying something different'.

Non-verbal signals

Body language is an important part of human interaction, but many people find the whole subject mystifying, if not sometimes rather mystical, and frustrating. Most of it is unconscious: we do not 'mean' to convey the message which our movement does convey. And we are often not consciously aware of messages we have picked up. We have all experienced people who made us feel uneasy or relaxed, wanted or rejected, without really being able to say why.

There is quite a lot we can do to control our own body language so that we do not give out negative signals. It is also worthwhile studying the body language of protagonists in negotiation to pick up how they are feeling about the situation. How are they reacting to different proposals and reactions of yours? Before we look briefly at the subject I must enter three important caveats.

1. Some body language is extremely subtle and both the signal and the reception are completely unconscious (except presumably to the expert). The pupils of the eyes are said to dilate with the pleasure of affectionate contact for example. Different emotions, such as fear, affection, anger and warmth, are said to produce different body odours. I must say for my own part that I have never been conscious of these reactions in myself or others and they are in the realm of pure theory for me.

2. Most body language is very easy to misinterpret even by those who have made a study of it. It is dangerous to rely on it by itself and especially so to over-interpret isolated movements. A gradually accruing pattern of behaviour will give you a lot more information about how a protagonist is feeling than a sudden movement.

I attended a communications course many years ago during which we observed our group behaviour on video. At one point I suddenly stiffened in my chair and arched backwards as though physically withdrawing from the group. All the observers interpreted the movement in that way. In fact I was simply reacting to a sudden jab of pain in my stomach, probably as a result of over-indulgence the evening before. It was nothing to do with the content of the meeting whatever.

3. Finally, over-concentration on your own and others' body language can produce a degree of self-consciousness which is self-defeating. Relax and smile: your body language will convey the message very effectively if you do.

With all these cautions, is the subject worth bothering with at all? Well, yes it is, because much of it is quite straightforward and very useful.

Relax

Before you go into a meeting make a conscious effort to relax. Sit in a comfortable chair; drop your shoulders; breathe easily and deeply, watching your stomach rise and fall. One minute of conscious relaxation will do a great deal to steady you. It is much more valuable than a frenetic, last-minute scramble to make sure that you have every last argument in place for the meeting.

Think positive

Yes, I know it is a cliché, but it is effective nevertheless. Remind yourself that you are good at what you do. You have something to offer which is valuable to the people you are going to meet. There is no reason to assume that they will not think so too. You feel relaxed and comfortable. You are going to make them feel relaxed and comfortable. You will smile at them and shake their hands warmly. Listen attentively to what they say. (And note it down if it is a key point: nothing wrong with doing that. It emphasises the importance you attached to them and their message.) Just remember that the people across the table are very important to you, as you are to them. You want them to reach agreement with you and the better you are able to convey their value to you in the way you relate to them, the more likely they are to do so.

If you find it difficult to relate to the previous two paragraphs, you might think about going on a short stress management course. There are books you can read, but because the subject is more about how you feel than what you think, many people find it better to learn to do it interactively. It is certainly related to personality but the important thing to grasp is that it is a *learned* technique.

Your body language

If you can convey this generally friendly ambience, details of your physical behaviour need not worry you too much. It is worth reviewing your own body movements nevertheless. 'Watch' yourself and your movements during different kinds of encounters. A lot of people begin meetings with their arms folded tightly across their chest: it looks very defensive even though it may not be meant to be. A friend of mine shakes her head gently from side to side in conversation: first impression is that she is disagreeing with what you say, but it is simply a mannerism. I have a tendency to put my hand up to my mouth and stroke my face:

it looks negative and reserved and I have to control it consciously. Ask a few people you trust, colleagues, partner, friends, if there is something that tends to strike them about your mannerisms. Do you do something which irritates? Do you sometimes look defensive and withdrawn? The point about all this is that non-verbal signals are easy to misinterpret. Individual mannerisms are unlikely to undermine a generally relaxed and friendly persona to any extent; but why not improve the chance of conveying those messages?

Good habits

Try to develop habits which become increasingly automatic and come into play in any interaction with others. Part of maturity is learning to build in compensations for our weaknesses. Someone with a short fuse has to control a tendency to loss of temper. Someone who tends to arrive late for meetings has to learn to manage time. You need to identify and control the mannerisms which may not be helping you. Develop the habit of checking every couple of minutes to identify and arrest them as they start to happen.

If you continue to work on your behaviour in this way for all kinds of meetings and social and business encounters, it becomes increasingly automatic. For heaven's sake don't wait until you are involved in a high profile crucial negotiation to start practising! You will have quite enough to worry about without being overly conscious about how you look as well. Once a habit takes hold it will become a natural part of negotiation as well other meetings.

Their body language

As the meeting progresses watch how they are responding to you. Are they fidgeting, looking away from you, shuffling papers, folding their arms and leaning back? You may be losing them if they are. Are you talking too much to regain their attention? What are you saying (or doing) which has caused them to start to react in this way? Are they giving you 'negative vibes'? Pursing the lips, screwing up the face, shaking the head: we all know the signals very well. Use them as cues to tell you how you are doing.

Tangents

Many of us tend to become distracted by our particular enthusiasms and some people tend to shoot constantly down tracks which are tangential to the main theme, simply because they are interesting. Passing references can help the discussion to flow. Whole sub-themes are usually distracting at least and can cause you to lose the central thread which is the real purpose of the meeting. If this is you, school yourself into thinking: 'Here I go again – how relevant is this to the subject?'

Many people in health and social services have strong moral, political or professional values. What do you do if your protagonist makes a racist or sexist aside? Do you confront it in the meeting and, by doing so, make it less likely that you will achieve your central objective? This kind of thing happens quite often. I am not offering you an answer to the question. But I am suggesting that you think through your own answer before you have to do so 'on your feet' in the middle of an important negotiation. You can't prepare for every eventuality, of course, but it does help to have given it some thought beforehand.

There are sometimes affronts to professional values too. They are by no means always intended aggressively or challengingly. Quite often they are merely thoughtless. Where do you stand on letting people get away with attitudes which you find total anathema?

Many years ago I had a minor operation. It took place under local anaesthetic and the surgeon decided to 'put me at my ease' while he worked by engaging me in conversation. He had obviously attended the Pol Pot school of diplomacy! The line which followed his discovery that I was a social worker by trade went something like this:

> The trouble with social workers is that they are usually scatty young women in beads and sandals and they don't know very much about anything. They have no experience of life and just bottle out when faced with anything amounting to a decision... Don't you agree?

You may imagine that I was very strongly moved to put him right with some force. While this was going on he was wielding a very sharp instrument over a part of my anatomy of which I was inordinately fond. I decided that the lesser good must give way to the greater and said nothing at all!

Handling aggression, stress and emotion

Emotional behaviour is often very difficult to manage and respond to, especially if it is sudden and unexpected. Some people use it quite deliberately to destabilise their protagonists and throw them off balance. Some men might concede another £5 per hour as a way of pacifying a copiously weeping female protagonist. Some people (men and women) might be intimidated from pressing their demands too assertively in the face of a red-faced and shouting male protagonist. Of course these sexual stereotypes are often reversed: men sometimes show great distress and women can be as aggressive and bullying as men.

The best ways of dealing with emotional reactions during negotiation are mostly by not reacting to them yourself.

1. Don't make an instant response. Without averting your eyes allow a short pause if you can. If the emotion is feigned it will indicate that you have not been thrown off-balance. If it is genuine it will allow the other person to regain composure.

2. Don't be 'clever' and assume you know whether the outburst is real or theatrical. If you say what you think, right or wrong, you will push the other person into a corner and make it difficult for him or her to back down without losing face.

3. Don't meet emotion with emotion. If you back down in the face of aggression or distress you are in effect losing your grip on the agenda. If you reciprocate 'How dare you speak to me in that tone', or 'I've got my problems too you know' there is a serious danger of a stand-off where everybody tends to stop listening to voices other than their own.

4. Don't lose sight of why you are there. Stick to the point as calmly and rationally as possible. But don't become too sententious and over-elaborate about it. To an angry person elaborate calmness and rationality can appear patronising and superior. It can serve to fuel feelings of inadequacy at having lost control and, paradoxically, make it worse. So 'superior' body language and the elaborate calmness and slowness which people sometimes adopt when talking to a naughty child are to be avoided too!

Men and women talking

When I read *You Just Don't Understand: Women and Men in Conversation* by Deborah Tannen it was a revelation to me. It helped me understand, for the first time, some of the cross-purpose conversations between men and women in particular with which I had been uncomprehendingly familiar.

Encapsulating a rich and interesting book in a paragraph or two is a risky business but I hope Ms Tannen will forgive me for trying. The central thesis is that, in addition to the messages contained in conversations, there are also 'metamessages' which signal the relationship which the protagonist is trying to establish and invite reciprocation. These signals are of two main kinds. The first are signals of solidarity, interdependence and (Tannen's word) 'intimacy'. The second are signals of hierarchy, leadership and independence. Everybody sends both types of signal from time to time but men tend to send and expect signals about independence and competition. Women tend to send and expect signals about interdependence and cooperation.

It explained for the first time some of the hitherto incomprehensible demands made by my wife during the quarter of a century we have been together. It also explained her occasional hurt and confusion at things I had said which had been intended to be helpful and supportive. I understood for the first time why my wife always wants to have a contact address and telephone number when I am away from home.

I used to find such questions irritating and intrusive; an invasion of my independence. As I saw it then, she wished to 'keep tabs on me' and monitor and control my freedom of movement. I tried to contain my irritation because I knew she found it hurtful and rejecting, but I had no idea why. She was actually signalling her wish to share in my experience and to be able to be in touch with me even when I was not there. For her it was an expression of care and an acknowledgement of our interdependence.

This 'distortion of transmission' is at its most stark between men and women, although it is by no means confined to exchanges between different genders. Imagine a telephone conversation in which some of the keywords which the listener hears are different from the words which the speaker speaks. That, in effect, is what differences of perception do. The following example taken from Tannen's book shows the contrasting impact of a conversation on the same subject first from shared then from different perceptions.

Eve had a lump removed from her breast. Shortly after the operation, talking to her sister, she said that she found it upsetting to have been cut into, and that looking at the stitches was distressing because they left a seam that had changed the contour of her breast. Her sister said 'I know. When I had my operation I felt the same way.' Eve made the same observation to her friend Karen, who said 'I know. It's like your body has been violated.' But when she told her husband, Mark, how she felt, he said, 'You can have plastic surgery to cover up your scar and restore the shape of your breast.'

Eve had been comforted by her sister and her friend, but she was not comforted by Mark's comment. Quite the contrary: it upset her more. Not only didn't she hear what she wanted, that he understood her feelings, but, far worse, she felt he was asking her to undergo more surgery just when she was telling him how much this operation had upset her.

The women were saying 'I know how you feel'. The man was saying 'I can fix that for you'. It is easy to imagine an equally frustrating encounter running in exactly the opposite direction: 'I come to you with a problem and all you can do is cap it with one of your own.'

It was not until a student on a course I was running some time after I read the book made some reference to its significance in negotiation that I began to think about it in that context. Is the overt message you are receiving from your protagonist being distorted by the way you receive it? Are you sure the message you are conveying is the one which is being received? When you give a signal which appears to be being rejected, is it the message itself or its implications for the relationship between you and the receiver which is causing the problem?

Earlier on I advocated the establishment of a relaxed and friendly rapport as a valuable aid to effective negotiation. But what if, in spite of all your friendly messages, the people across the table remain stiff, formal and unsmiling? What is going on? They may actually be threatened by your informality. It may feel like a threat to their independence and to introduce uncertainty into your relative positions. Your familiarity shows that you do not know your (inferior) place. Alternatively, you are patronising them in an attempt to establish your (superior) place.

I visited a colleague with whom I had had a friendly relationship for many years. The business purpose of the visit was an exploratory meeting to discuss the possibility of the organisation for which he worked contracting with me to do some work for them. He had recently had some acutely distressing news concerning a member of his family. I was anxious to empathise with him and to allow him, if he wished, to talk about how he was feeling. He was a friend and I wanted to help if I could.

During the course of the meeting I introduced the subject several times. Each time I was curtly rebuffed. 'That is not what we are here to talk about.' His conduct of what we were there to talk about felt aggressive and hostile and included warnings that if I worked for them they would watch me like a hawk and come down on me like a ton of bricks if I did not deliver as expected. From someone I had worked with closely for almost twenty years, and from whom I had thought professional respect was reciprocated, this felt deeply wounding.

At the time I thought that I was simply the butt of his anger and distress at what had happened, but I now think I actually caused the problem. My well-meaning signal of solidarity with a friend in distress was not received like that. I was adopting the caring 'parent figure' rôle; putting myself in a superior position to him. How could he possibly negotiate professionally from a position of such weakness? He had to put me in my place. His private distress was nothing to do with me. I was there to get favours from him; not the other way round.

Other tools for understanding and managing behaviour

A friend of mine has an amusing aphorism: 'If the only tool you have is a hammer, it's surprising how many problems look like nails!' We certainly do have a tendency to try to use a new trick we have just learned for things for which it was never intended. First-year psychology students, on learning about 'defence mechanisms', are often tempted for a time to interpret almost all human behaviour in this way.

Among the helping professions however the problem is often the very opposite. Most of us have a huge toolkit for working with people; a great many tricks. Some of the more sophisticated tools are specific for use in a given situation, but many of them are not. They are simply applied relationship management skills. You will be using these skills, as managers, supervisors and professionals, in your day-to-day work. For some reason it is difficult to transpose ideas from one context to another; to extrapolate the learning. Perhaps we store our skills in bundles in our minds. 'When I am being a social worker I need to get out my social work bundle. When I am being a manager I can put my social work bundle away and get out my management bundle. When I am negotiating I need to get out my negotiation bundle. But hold on; my negotiation bundle is only small and part-filled!'

Perhaps we need to think about our skills more flexibly than that. The skills we use for negotiating in daily life can be applied to more formal negotiating contexts. The skills we learned to help us function as social workers, doctors, psychologists, nurses or managers can be used across these boundaries and to undertake other tasks like negotiation. Sometimes the skills need to be modified for a different use. As a negotiator you are not a therapist for example. Sometimes they need no modification at all: a 'good bedside manner' which puts people at ease is equally useful in many situations. You just need to make the mental jump to apply it.

Once their relevance had occurred to me, I could make use of the ideas I had gained from reading Tannen in the context of negotiation. Many years ago a colleague of mine made an equally sudden extrapolation of her skills.

In 1971 I worked as an area social services officer in a London borough, just after the new social services departments had been formed. In those days there was a lot of heady nonsense about. Everybody thought they could do everything equally well. Former child care officers started working with elderly people as though they had been doing it all their lives. I was talking about the admission of an old lady to an old people's home with one of the social workers who had been, until a few months before, a very skilled child care officer.

I was making clear, as kindly as I could, that her handling of the process had been crass and bureaucratic, but I was making very little progress. Until I said to her 'You would never admit a child like that, would you?' She looked appalled. No of course she wouldn't; it would have been unthinkable.

Transactional analysis, systems theory, learning theory, various models of human growth and development, cognitive therapy, team management and problem-solving models all have useful applications to the negotiating mode of human interaction. Many readers will already have an idea, at least in outline, of what most of these frameworks mean. Within your reference group, however, you will probably have people with a deep knowledge of one or two of them. Why not do an audit of the skills you already have collectively and consider how they can be more widely shared within the group? Think about what insights one may gain from applying the knowledge to the particular situation of negotiation. And think about how the skills learned for another application might be useful in this one.

Key learning points

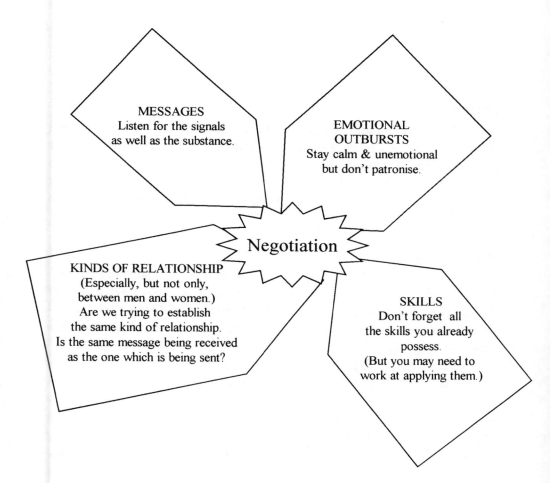

Figure 6.2

7. Opportunities and Disasters

Introduction

In this chapter we consider how to make the best use of the opportunities inherent in the situation, and some of the dangers which attend them. We look at the balance of power between the two sides in negotiation, and discuss how to manage it and influence the balance in your favour. Finally, since however carefully you prepare, things will go wrong, we consider a few ways to snatch success from the jaws of disaster!

Opportunities

Everyone who has ever been on even a half-day management course knows about SWOT analysis. This involves considering the situation, project, negotiation or deal in terms of its Strengths/Weaknesses/Opportunities/Threats. The matrix I introduced earlier in the book (in Chapters 2 and 5) is in essence a negotiation-focused SWOT analysis.

There are always two groups of people to consider in a negotiation: the people immediately in front of you; and the people behind them, their constituents. The people you face across the table may be very similar to you, they may have the same profession and similar aspirations and outlook as you. It is a golden opportunity to find agreement. But don't forget that the people to whom they account, and those to whom you account, may be very different from both of you and from each other.

The opposite is also possible. The people you face across the table may be very different, or very hostile to you but you (or your constituents) may be able to relate well to theirs. Consider the two examples below. The first is an extremely common one in the health and social services fields: co-professionals negotiating on behalf of different organisations. The second case is a direct appeal to (key members of) a constituency outside the negotiating forum.

Co-professionals negotiating together

I once saw a film about the cold war which was unmemorable in every respect save for one line. At the end of a high-level meeting between the Soviet and American sides an American general concludes by saying 'So we'd better have your German scientists talk to our German scientists to see what they can come up with.'

The implication of this little vignette is that the nuclear scientists on both sides are exclusively of German origin whichever constituency they work for. In the film, the scientists meet to negotiate a *modus vivendi* between the two sides. They speak the same language, in every sense. They may even have trained or worked together. They understand the issues at stake more thoroughly than anybody else. However they represent different constituencies which are, in this case, bitter enemies.

For a similar case, much closer to home and our own experiences, consider a meeting between a health authority and an NHS trust. If the intended outcome has any direct health implications there will be doctors present on both sides of the table. They will probably know each other professionally, and perhaps socially, and they will speak the same language. They too represent different constituencies. They do not regard each other as enemies – at least, one hopes not! – and they are both part of the NHS. But they have different purposes and different tasks and, although under a broad umbrella, they are accountable to different people.

It is a great help if the protagonists in negotiation speak the same language, have a similar knowledge base, similar attitudes and values and mutual respect. Chapters Eight and Nine are largely about developing common ground through better mutual understanding. Doctors like to negotiate with doctors because they know where they are coming from professionally. There are no doctors in most social services departments, so any dialogue between health and social services has to start by establishing mutual trust and understanding between professionals who are different.

Common language and perception facilitates communication as long as you keep the needs of the different constituencies in mind. If you lose sight of the (constituency) interests you represent it can be a problem. As a professional in the Civil Service I was sometimes approached by voluntary organisations wanting to develop services or projects. Knowing my professional background and interests they usually assumed (usually correctly) that I was sympathetic to the cause which they espoused. Most of them were fully aware of my locus in relation to decisions about their proposal but a few lost sight of it. Expressions like 'we are all on the same side' showed very clearly that they had not begun to consider the context in which I worked nor the agenda of those to whom I was accountable. Identifying me as an 'ally' actually hindered their ability to develop strong arguments. They expected me to do it for them.

Working together to produce agreement

Protagonists in negotiation may sometimes find themselves effectively working together to construct a case which will be acceptable to their respective constituencies. There is always a delicate ethical line to tread here. If the debate is about finding trade-offs with which both sides can live, or expressing the proposed deal in words which are politically acceptable to both sides, then that is not merely legitimate but laudable. However, if it involves one side or the other suppressing some aspects of the information in order to produce agreement 'back at the ranch' then it is not legitimate. 'All professions are conspiracies against the laity' said one of George Bernard Shaw's characters in 'The Doctor's Dilemma' (Act I). It is a real and ever-present temptation to 'edit' difficult and controversial aspects of things and to justify it on the grounds that 'members won't understand the full implications'. The ethical legitimacy of such conclusions is always open to question. And, from an entirely pragmatic point of view, there is a serious danger the agreement will unravel in the end once the members (or whoever else it is) start to understand the full implications!

A training agency was running a series of seminars for the members of new unitary local authorities to help familiarise them with their recently acquired responsibilities for social services. In the negotiation for one of these seminars, the director wanted to play down one aspect of the seminar which focused on the dilemmas and options which members face, on the ground that he was best placed to tell them which options they should choose. Helping them to understand where they had choice would make his already difficult life virtually impossible.

You would need to have a lot more detail to draw any conclusion about the ethics of the director's stance but the pragmatic issue is clear enough, even on this information. If it had gone ahead as he wished, the director would have done himself few favours. Some member would probably have caught wind of the intention to exclude the 'options' session from somewhere. The seminar had already been run several times with it in.

Going over the head of your protagonist

A businessman owned several nursing homes and old peoples' homes and wanted to reach an agreement for all of them with his local social services department. He thought he could offer consistency, a high standard of care, explicit assurances of quality and, given the size of his operation, a flexible response to a wide range of needs. In return he sought a pricing agreement and a minimum market share.

He met first the responsible assistant director then, on reaching impasse with her, the director herself. He fared no better with the director who supported the position taken by her assistant: spot purchase of beds at the standard authority determined rate: take it or leave it!

He felt very strongly that they were rejecting the idea of a deal on the basis of a prejudice about him and his kind of operation without any regard to what he had to offer. The assistant director had made a number of rather snide comments during the course of the meetings which supported that view. So he pulled strings. He knew a few councillors and, to cut a long story short, the director finally reached an agreement with him, under pressure.

When the businessman told me this story he finished by saying 'I won of course; but I may not have done. And, in the process of getting my way, I made at least two implacable enemies in key positions to do me harm. I don't think I would do the same thing again.'

The lessons from this case don't need to be laboured. Don't do this kind of thing unless you feel you have no choice! Actually the problem arose largely because of the order of events. Consider what might have happened if the businessman had known in advance how the assistant director felt about private enterprise care by, for example, sounding out his staff about their experience of her.

He may have concluded that it would not be sensible to approach someone with an offer she was predisposed to refuse without preparing the ground first. Instead of asking his councillor contacts to knock heads together, he might have talked about the general idea of a deal which would be good for the council and good for him. Having got them interested he then might have asked them to facilitate a meeting with officers to see if this good idea in principle could be worked out in practice. It might have worked out much the same in the end of course, but I think you will agree that the odds would have been shifted significantly.

A colleague reading the previous two paragraphs commented that it seemed to him 'unethical – or even crooked' to behave like that. I leave you to judge but I cannot see it that way. Who is the victim? Who has been exploited unfairly? Saying one thing to one person and something which conflicts with it to another *is* unethical (at least in my opinion). On the other hand, handling transactions in the most advantageous order is, again in my opinion, the exercise of skill and judgement. It is one more example of how careful preparation and good intelligence can contribute enormously to the prospect of success. The buzz word for this kind of process is 'networking', which might be defined as 'making, and making use of, a wide range of contacts to further your business objectives'. The word tends to carry a rather vague, almost mystical aura. On the contrary, the subject repays systematic attention. An excellent recent publication is *Effective Networking for Professional Success* by Rupert Hart. It is a little book; you will be able to read it in a morning. Like almost all of its kind, it is written with the commercial provider primarily in mind but it contains some excellent ideas that you can apply, simply expressed.

Don't exploit the other side's weakness

There is an important distinction to be made between driving a hard bargain and taking unfair advantage, and there is an ethical judgement to be made about what is 'fair' and what is not which we all have to exercise for ourselves. There are, however, pragmatic reasons for not exploiting your protagonist's weakness. It is one 'opportunity' which is almost always illusory and to be avoided.

If you are selling illegal video tapes at a car boot sale, exploiting the punters' gullibility and lack of sense of value (or just plain lack of sense) can pay handsome dividends. But don't bring these dubious talents to work on Monday morning. Taking advantage of your protagonist's poor negotiating skills or their lack of sense may do you as much harm in the end as it does them.

Over lunch during a seminar for a voluntary organisation one of the participants said to me, 'Of course the problem is that you will run courses like this for local authority people too, then we will be back where we started.' I think he was wrong. Effective negotiation is the process of reaching an agreement which is acceptable to both sides as fair and reasonable and the best they can get under the circumstances. The best way to achieve that is for the representatives of *both* sides to be knowledgeable and skilful. If that is not the case in reality, those who are skilful need to help those who are not in the way they conduct themselves. It can be a very uncomfortable position to be in. The bank manager who is simultaneously negotiating for the bank and trying to represent the interests of the incompetent customer fairly is in an awkward spot indeed.

By no means everyone agrees with this perception of the negotiator's rôle. *Caveat emptor* (let the buyer beware) is an aphorism which goes back to Roman times. We could have a fine debate about the code of ethics to which, for example, the used-car dealer should subscribe; but there are sensible market reasons why he should not want the customer to feel ripped off, the week after making his or her purchase.

If that is true in a bilateral commercial transaction, how much more true is it when both groups of protagonists are public servants. If the negotiation fails to achieve the best result, the principal loser is the public.

Even when one half of the bargain is a commercial supplier, fairness is important. If the example I gave from a simulation exercise where the 'director of social services' managed to wrong-foot the 'home owners' had been for real it would have been unfair. For a monopoly purchaser, as the social services department is in such a case, there is a real dilemma. Don't push hard enough and the providers do not give good value for money. Push too hard and standards fall or businesses fail. The difficulty is in finding the right balance. The point is that gaining an advantage which arises from the negotiating incompetence of one side seldom achieves more than a short-term gain. A hard bargain, skilfully fought for on both sides, offers the best prospect for both.

Power issues

The balance of power

A negotiation would not be taking place at all unless there might be something in it for both sides, but it is often very difficult to remember that. There is a tendency in most of us to feel that the people on the other side of the table are more powerful than we are. 'We need them more than they need us.' In fact, however, the very purpose of negotiation is the mutual satisfaction of need. The people sitting opposite you would not be there unless they wanted something. It pays to remember that.

There are, nevertheless, some inequalities of power in most negotiating relationships. They are not necessarily all on one side of the table. One side can be strong in some respects and weak in others and that, as we have seen elsewhere, can be the source of some useful trade-offs.

In addition to these 'natural' inequalities there are several ploys which people use to increase their relative status.

Pulling rank

Pulling rank is an extremely frequent tactic. I suspect it is much more often a statement about self-aggrandisement than a conscious ploy to gain a negotiating advantage. Whatever the intention, it can put you at a serious disadvantage unless you are prepared for it; and it can wreck the negotiation to nobody's advantage if it is handled badly.

Of course, people are sometimes in a very powerful position by the nature of their office, their buying power, their expert knowledge, their experience, their contacts, or their influence. That is presumably why you are talking to them. Why are they talking to you? Because you too have power vested in the thing they want from you. It is helpful to remember that when someone starts pulling rank. The responses in brackets to the following comments are what you should remember. They are emphatically not what you should say out loud.

- '*I am the Director of Social Services in this authority. People have to listen to me.*' (But they don't have to do what he says and neither do you, without something in return.)

- '*I have a budget of £29 million. I can buy any amount of what you are offering for two-thirds of the price you are asking.*' (What has the first statement got to do with the second? Don't forget that economies of scale do not work in quite the same way for services as they do for goods.)

- '*I wrote a thesis on this subject. I take it you have read [mentions abstruse and erudite tome].*' (The real meaning of this is 'I take it you have *not* read…'. This is often one to confront – but only if you are knowledgeable about the subject yourself. It really depends on whether this expertise is what you are offering. If it is, you are in trouble if you can't deal on equal terms! But more often that not you will be offering something different. Be careful not to lose sight of it under the onslaught of erudition. As an information management consultant I am often bombarded by 'techie speak' from IT people. Until you learn to live with it, it can feel very de-skilling.)

- '*Listen, sonny, I have been doing this job for twenty years.*' (It really does happen! Why is he saying this? It may be that he is afraid that something you will say will call into question the value of what he has been doing for twenty years. Aggressive lines like this do tempt you to land a verbal punch on the nose. Don't deliver one! He is actually feeling very vulnerable already. If you threaten him any more you will lose any chance of getting what you want from him.)

- '*I was saying to the Secretary of State that we should do this only last week.*' (You are meant to be impressed. So let them think you are impressed; where is the harm? As long as you do not allow yourself to feel that it somehow reduces your significance, which is seldom the intention, it is most unlikely to damage your negotiating position. If you sneer at such name-dropping you will gain nothing and may lose a great deal.)

- '*Leave it with me. I'll see what I can do.*' (If this is from someone you know well and trust it may mean something. Otherwise beware; the line is usually intended to imply serious influence and is usually meaningless. Ask yourself why she should be prepared to 'see what she can do' on your behalf. You might take it more seriously if 'it' will advance both your causes at once. But my advice is to keep your expectations severely in check and do not offer to do anything in return for such vague promises.)

Personal power

One of the most difficult things to resist is personal charisma. You want to do what this person suggests because the way he puts it, it seems so right. And you do not want to be the one to dash his hopes, so gracefully expressed. You must keep an eye on your agenda and hold fast to what you want from the negotiation. It can be very difficult: you may be seduced for a while and then need to retrench. If that happens don't let yourself become angry with him for having charmed you. It is your fault and you must put it right calmly, rationally and with as much good grace as you, in your turn, can muster.

Rôle power

People sometimes confuse what they do with who they are. Some of those in powerful positions come to believe that the power they possess is invested in themselves rather than the office they hold. Some become bullying or at least discourteous. Some become know-alls, 'experts on everything'. Some become control freaks, doling out information to their staff and others on a 'need to know' basis (which usually means 'don't need to know').

If you encounter such behaviour what do you do? By far the most important thing to do is not to believe it yourself. Your protagonist may have a higher status within his or her organisation than you do in yours, but you are negotiating on an equal footing. If you are not there is something wrong with the way the negotiation has been set up. It seldom pays to confront pompous, discourteous or bullying behaviour or to outsmart know-all behaviour. It is never wise to back down and become defensive and overawed in the face of such onslaughts. The best way to ensure that you do not get trapped by such behaviour is to recognise it for what it is.

Caught unprepared or unawares

Careful preparation helps you to spot the elephant traps and a large part of this book is about preparation and planning. But the unexpected will happen however well you prepare, and the inexperienced negotiator can become lulled into thinking that every eventuality has been covered. The shock of the completely unexpected is all the greater when it happens.

The unexpected can happen when your protagonists put on the table a whole new aspect which you had not thought about or could not have anticipated. It can happen if one of your team begins behaving in an unforeseen way. Your whole strategy can begin to unravel before your eyes if, say, it becomes plain that your primary objective in calling the meeting is a non-starter. Finally, your protagonists can respond to your proposal in a completely unexpected way.

> A social worker was concerned about a child who had been excluded from school. He thought it was a very damaging experience for an already disturbed child and seemed unjustified under the circumstances. Having drawn a blank with the head teacher he went to see the district education officer, who was not unsympathetic but said he would need something in writing from the social services department in order to act.
>
> For reasons which do not concern the story the director of social services learned of the problem and sent a note to the team leader. She wanted to discuss it with him and the social worker 'to decide how best to handle it'. The social worker, the team leader and the head of adolescent services spent some time discussing the possible options for getting things moving, in preparation for the meeting with the director.
>
> At the meeting with the director her significant opening line was 'Just drop this. You are putting some delicate negotiations with the education department in jeopardy here and I want this matter put on ice. OK?' That was the one line they had not prepared for. They had assumed that the director had wanted to help them find the best solution to the problem. They were 'up the creek without a paddle'.

One reason it is so important to review the negotiation after it has taken place is that you can learn from the unexpected and use the knowledge in future planning. These reviews will sometimes show that there are some things you will never be able to plan for however much time and experience you bring to bear. Was this case one of them? The question the social worker, team leader and head of adolescent services didn't ask themselves was 'Why does the director want to get involved in an individual case like this?' Had they done so they may have concluded that there was something more than the individual case involved.

Reviewing negotiations is all very well for learning for the next time, of course; but it does not get you out of the hole you have just fallen into here and now!

'Don't panic'

From *Dad's Army* to *The Hitchhiker's Guide to the Galaxy* this is the standard comic response to the unexpected. It is comic because nobody ever *chooses* to panic. There are, however, things you can do to manage your panic when it happens.

Animals and birds respond in one of three basic ways: freeze, fight or flee. Because we have the power of speech we add a fourth option to the repertoire: gabble (Figure 7.1). I don't panic in a group situation very often but when I do I produce the same basic response every time. I believe that this is true of most people, so it is helpful to think back to how you respond *immediately* to threat from someone else.

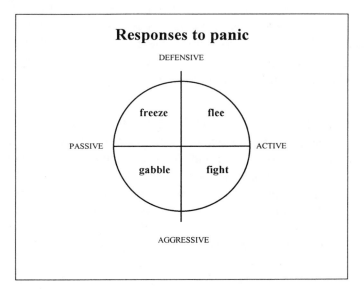

Figure 7.1

Passive responses

If you tend to have a passive response to panic it is a lot easier to manage than an active response. Passive responses leave you with more internal tension to cope with but tend to do a lot less damage, even if completely unchecked, than active ones.

If you tend to **freeze,** this may not do much to relieve your tension but it is the instinctive response which requires least management. You are not going to blurt out something you will regret because it will take you a few seconds to say anything at all. Your mind has gone blank, your throat has gone dry and, in extreme cases, your vision has gone temporarily blurred. Don't speak until your mind comes back, and even then not for another few seconds while you decide on an appropriate response. It may seem like an eternity to you but it does not usually seem the same to your protagonists. Unbelievably, the (subjectively) long silence can appear quite powerful.

> On two separate occasions, when I was still quite young and junior, a proposal I made in a meeting was the subject of a vitriolic outburst from a powerful figure much more senior than me. The responses were completely unexpected (and actually completely inappropriate too). On both occasions I was overawed and stunned by the force of the blow. I simply sat in silence, appalled and unable to speak. This was interpreted by others at the meeting as an eloquent assertion of the legitimacy of my position! I may have been thinking 'Please don't hit me again!', but what they, and presumably the offender, 'heard' was 'You may be in a more powerful position than me but my case is sound – and you know it.'

Aficionados of that great television classic *Yes, Minister* will have enjoyed Sir Humphrey under pressure. His syntax becomes more and more convoluted, his words become longer and longer and the whole thing is completely devoid of substantive meaning. People who are 'never lost for words' appear to be particularly prone to **gabble**. Gabble appears to be culturally determined. In my area of South Wales it becomes more lyrical, mystical and musical as it develops, and almost always ends with the mysterious phrase 'But we're getting there.'

This condition is a good deal less damaging than fight or flight, if only because the words seldom have any meaning at all. But if you tend to respond like this, try to stop it: it appears weak and your panic is obvious. If your protagonists are trying to get the better of you, you will have given them a good opening. Perhaps you have the ability to leave your mouth in gear while your brain is working, but most people cannot do this. They need to be briefly silent in order to think. The final grave disadvantage of this response to pressure is that it actually seems to increase one's level of anxiety, perhaps by deferring the opportunity to think constructively of a rational response.

Active responses

I know of at least one case of a physical assault in a meeting, and of several when people got up and stumped out. These are obviously disastrous reactions and even their verbal equivalents are singularly unhelpful. 'How dare you threaten us with this!' or (to one of your own team) 'Why didn't you find out about this?' And, equivalent to physical flight: 'I'm not standing for this!' or, less aggressively but worse still 'OK, we agree, anything you want.' If your analysis of past panic reactions lead you to conclude that they are something like this, prepare yourself for the possibility in the next meeting. Breathe evenly, sit quietly, let others do the talking and *be quiet* until the red haze or the blue funk has cleared.

Losing the way and finding it again

If it is clear that either you personally, or your entire team, have completely lost the agenda it will be sensible at least to seek an adjournment or maybe even to postpone the meeting altogether. If the other side proposes some major new points which you need to consider with constituents who are not present at the meeting, then those are obvious options.

Of course, life is never simple. You may need to take on board some major new issue without checking back because the time to reach an agreement is limited. Indeed, a common negotiating trick is to withhold a salient piece of information until the eleventh hour in order to wrong-foot the other side. It is not good practice to do this in my view, but not everyone plays by the same rules! Another negotiating trick is to set different members of the other side off in different, preferably conflicting, directions. If one of these tricks has destabilised you, you *must* regroup your ideas. Even if you cannot ask for a postponement you must at least seek an adjournment so that your team can decide exactly how to handle the new situation.

Working alone, working together

The situation does not depend on you alone. You may have lost your place but other members of your team might be well in control. You cannot rehearse the point at which the others take over if the lead spokesperson is fading, but you can give each other explicit permission, before the meeting, to pick up relevant threads which seem to be being dropped. An experienced team can become very skilled at passing the baton from one to the other in such a way that the protagonists are scarcely aware that it is happening.

If you are negotiating by yourself and crash, so to speak, the position is often irrecoverable without a pause. In that situation it is sometimes more difficult to ask for an adjournment unless you are robust enough to say 'I need time to think.' Perhaps you need a device: a natural break, time to make a phone call or two.

This does have some implications for how you set up your side of a negotiation. Even for people who work from the same office base it is more than twice as expensive to send two people to a meeting and more than three times to send three. Cost and effectiveness need to be kept in balance. It may be a lot more effective to send three people to negotiate a well-prepared and well-argued case. Individuals dashing from one ill-prepared meeting to another may achieve very little.

Key learning points

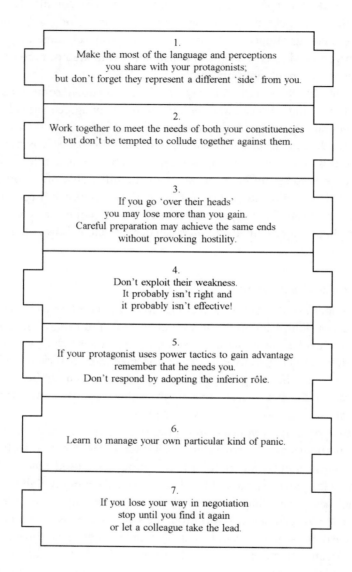

1.
Make the most of the language and perceptions
you share with your protagonists;
but don't forget they represent a different 'side' from you.

2.
Work together to meet the needs of both your constituencies
but don't be tempted to collude together against them.

3.
If you go 'over their heads'
you may lose more than you gain.
Careful preparation may achieve the same ends
without provoking hostility.

4.
Don't exploit their weakness.
It probably isn't right and
it probably isn't effective!

5.
If your protagonist uses power tactics to gain advantage
remember that he needs you.
Don't respond by adopting the inferior rôle.

6.
Learn to manage your own particular kind of panic.

7.
If you lose your way in negotiation
stop until you find it again
or let a colleague take the lead.

Figure 7.2

Part II

8.   The NHS and Social Services

Introduction

This chapter is a brief description of the most complex range of services in any post-industrial society. I haven't attempted to cover all of them but to focus instead on those aspects of the two services which interface with each other to the greatest extent. For that reason you will find almost nothing here about the huge changes in technology and professional practice which are accompanying the organisational changes to which I refer.

Ideally the chapter should be a loose-leaf insert into the book because both services are changing so rapidly that any description is only a freeze-frame of a particular moment. Even the government has difficulty keeping pace. When I was working on the first draft of the book (mid-1997, but after the election) the NHS Executive's World Wide Web site on the Internet provided 'A Guide to the National Health Service'. Many of the pages in that guide, and elsewhere on the site, talked about changes which *will take place* in 1995.

When negotiating with others it is wise to know as much as possible about the people you are talking to and their business. It shows you take them seriously. It helps them to take you seriously. All negotiation is about meeting other people's needs in exchange for having some of your own met, so it makes sense to be as clear as you can about what their needs are. I hope the chapter will help you to fill gaps in your knowledge. Many readers will be familiar with much of it and I ask for your indulgence if I have missed areas which you consider important, and especially if you discover any mistakes of fact. Please let me know if you do.

The direction in which health and welfare services are moving

Ten years ago

Ten years ago there was less privately run health and social care in Britain than today. Most of it then was independent of the local authorities which ran public social services and of the National Health Service. The NHS and the social services departments inspected the independent hospitals, nursing homes, residential homes and day nurseries which constituted the larger part of this provision. However, with certain exceptions, they did not contract with them to provide services. From the point of view of the establishments, the health authorities and the social services departments were bureaucratic controllers rather than customers with cash to spend.

There were certainly many services provided to the social services and the NHS by the private and voluntary sectors, including some professional services. Using agency nurses was a well-established means of filling gaps and employing agency social workers was becoming more popular. Voluntary children's homes and schools run by charitable foundations and, to some extent, commercially run children's homes and schools had long been used by local authority social services departments; many local voluntary services were supported and funded by social services departments.

Negotiation about these services was very limited. Costs tended to be fixed by formula or by scarcity alone. Discussion about the content and quality of the service was remarkably limited. Contracts were ritual texts: full of long words and legal phrases and devoid of real meaning. To some extent they still are, in spite of all the changes.

Recent changes

It is hard to overstate but easy to oversimplify the changes which have taken place during the past ten years. They have implications for every kind of interaction involving the various components of the NHS, other health service providers, the public, private and voluntary social service providers and the local authorities as social services commissioners and providers. The health authorities (commissioners) and the NHS trusts (providers) need to negotiate with each other. Both need to negotiate with the local authorities about the boundaries between their services, about effective collaboration in the way they are delivered and a myriad of other issues. Given the size and scope of many of the services involved in these processes it is a matrix of mind-numbing complexity.

The functions of the NHS have been separated. There are now commissioning health authorities and service providing trusts which include hospitals, community based health services and, for example, ambulance services. GP fund-holding has been introduced. Since the change of government in May 1998 more structural and organisational changes have been proposed, but they have yet to take place. Perhaps the two most important are the proposed merger of some of the trusts into larger units and the replacement of fund-holding GPs with commissioning GPs.

Even before the change of government, the notion of open market competition among the trusts for the business being offered by the authorities was in decline. Trusts were enjoined to cooperate with each other to provide efficent services rather than to compete regardless of need. The proposal to increase their size is a further logical step along that road.

The proposal to establish GP commissioning groups is very recent: in essence it is that they should join forces and become commissioning teams. It is too early to know what its implications will be in practice, but it is clear that the new government wants to continue the trend towards giving the GPs a more and more pivotal role in determining the shape of local health services.

The previous government put increasing pressure on local authorities to become enablers rather than service providers, and to separate their own organisations into purchasing and service providing divisions. So far there is no sign of the new government wishing to change that. Since the early 1990s there has been a statutory requirement for the social services and health to negotiate joint community care and children's services plans. Although these changes have been taking place over the past ten years the pace has accelerated lately, and most of them have actually begun to bite only within the past five years or less.

The justification for the changes was that they would lead to better patient care and greater client choice. By separating needs assessment and commissioning from service provision there would be greater clarity and responsibility, clearer accountability and more transparency. The same broad justification was used for the changes in both services, but the changes which took place within the two services were not remotely similar to each other.

Notably, 'commissioning' of social services provision is done at individual level, based on a personal assessment, while in the NHS, it is based on the perceived health care needs of the whole population living within the catchment area of the health authority. Provision of health services, on the other hand, is largely done within the NHS itself. Social services are provided by a much greater mix of public/private/voluntary sector services.

These changes are gradually settling down, but they have not been universally welcomed by the public or the professions. The public perception of a failing health service almost certainly contributed to the heavy defeat on the Conservative Government in the elections of May 1997. (Social services have a very low public profile in spite of the fact that they are very large spenders of public finance.) A quick browse through the pages of *Community Care*, the leading British social services weekly journal, shows a profession deeply uneasy with its lot and with the way social services have been developing. This was especially true during the year immediately before the election.

Enthusiasm for the changes is not unbounded among health care professionals either. A former chair of the British Medical Association, Jeremy Lee-Potter has just (1997) produced a scholarly but scathing indictment of the reforms in the NHS *A Damn Bad Business: the NHS Deformed*. His central point is that a major structural change of dubious provenance was introduced across the whole country without any piloting.

Many professionals are confused about the changes which are taking place in their own service and even more confused about what is happening in the other one. This has a profound effect on their ability to function effectively as negotiators. Clarity about who you are, whom you represent and what you want are crucial to negotiating effectiveness. A good understanding of where your protagonist is coming from and what she is likely to want is almost as important.

Consider the following example. This case is from social services, but the same kind of misunderstanding can occur within the health sphere or across the boundary between the two.

A meeting takes place between a local authority and a large charity which provides a range of services. The charity's representatives think of themselves as representing an organisation with experience, authority and resources. They can command a legitimate position as a partner with the local authority to plan and contribute to the shape and policy of the service which is under discussion.

The local authority representatives think of themselves as representing an organisation which has made all the relevant policy decisions already, and they carry the democratic mandate to implement those policies without reference to others in their own area. They regard the charity as merely a possible service provider: one of several from whom they might purchase a service from both the voluntary and commercial sectors.

Unless the two sides at least understand their respective perceptions the dialogue will be fruitless and acrimonious: the middle ground between two unknown points is impossible to find!

It is just this kind of mutual misperception which is generated by rapidly changing cultures. This of course is not an argument for no change, nor even for slow change. But it is vital that changing perceptions are communicated honestly and openly if effective dialogue is to be possible.

An overview of the health service

Purpose

> The fundamental purpose of the NHS is to secure through the resources available the greatest possible improvement in the physical and mental health of the people of England by promoting health, preventing ill health, diagnosing and treating injury and disease and caring for those with long-term illness and disability who require the services of the NHS. Alan Langlands, NHS Chief Executive, England; Foreword to *A Guide to the National Health Service*, NHS Executive 1995, p.2.

Anyone who is negotiating with, or on behalf of, the NHS would be well advised to memorise that statement of purpose (or its similar Welsh, Scottish or Northern Irish equivalent). You should think about its implications for the particular subject under consideration. That is what the NHS is about: the Chief Executive has publicly said so.

If you are negotiating *for* the NHS, are your protagonists trying to push you into fields of activity which do not fit with the statement? If you are negotiating *with* the NHS do your protagonists seem to be overlooking their responsibilities, as implied by the statement? Under the day-to-day pressure of trying to make ends meet it is easy to lose sight of strategic objectives. Some of the endless debates between the NHS and the local authorities about responsibility for continuing care might make better progress if each started from the first principles embodied in the statement.

The Chief Executive may have intended the order of his words to be significant, but it bears little relation to actual spending priorities. His order was:

- promoting,
- preventing,
- diagnosing,
- treating,
- caring.

The order of expenditure is:

- treating,
- diagnosing,
- promoting,
- preventing.

Caring seems now to be regarded as largely the responsibility of others, notably the social services.

Ever since its creation, critics of the NHS have claimed that it should really be called the National Sickness Service. If levels of expenditure are equated with levels of importance – and, in political terms at least, they are – health promotion and prevention are very small beer by comparison with the sickness services. Whether the NHS should take a more proactive rôle in both these activities, and be allocated the public resources to do so, is a political rather than a professional question. I imagine very few readers will take issue with me for saying that the NHS is seriously under-resourced for what it already does. The statement of purpose, however laudable, does not generate another pound but, as a negotiator, you might find it useful as a lever to move the pounds around a little! Which of the issues in the statement you bring strongly into play depends, of course, on the case you are making at the time.

Who is the NHS for?

The NHS is a universal service, available to everyone. Most of us only see the small part of it which affects us as patients. But the great majority has a constant reminder of the existence of the service by actually using it, even if only as a result of the occasional visit to our GP.

A national service

The NHS, as its name implies, is a national service. The Secretaries of State for Health, Scotland, Wales and Northern Ireland are directly accountable to Parliament for the standards and funding of the service. The health authorities are responsible for providing 'services sensitive to local needs' but they are responsible to the relevant Secretary of State. They might provide locally sensitive services, but they are certainly not locally accountable for them.

Organisation

A service in transition

The NHS is one of the biggest employers in Europe, and an organisation as large as this is bound to be complex. It is at least possible that there are some very large organisations with many functions which nobody fully understands. If that is true, the NHS must be one of them. It was never easy to understand but doing so has been made much more difficult by the sheer pace of change.

Nothing stands still, of course, but very large bureaucracies used to modify at a stately pace. Sometimes structures would change, but day-to-day procedures would take time to follow. Sometimes the reverse would happen. Changes in the real world would produce changes in operational responses, but the organisation would take time to assimilate what was happening.

In my youth those long school photographs were produced by a camera which swept round a semi-circle of children. A favourite trick was for some little devil at one end to run round to the other and pop up again. The reforms of the NHS have gathered such pace during the past ten years that it is virtually impossible to produce an accurate snapshot any longer. If you used one of those old cameras to photograph the NHS, things would keep popping up all over the place!

This pace of change is deeply unsettling for those working within it. Even if the change itself is in the right direction it creates pressure and dislocation. For the negotiator the essential thing is to be clear about your locus and objectives and not allow the maelstrom to undermine your own clarity. If you are negotiating with, or within, the health service bear in mind that the people facing you may be vague themselves about the detailed implications of some of the changes.

Health authorities

The chairs and non-executive members of the health authorities are appointed by the secretaries of state and they are funded by central government. This is a source both of strength and weakness. On the one hand, the authorities are not subject to the caprice of local political whim as local authorities sometimes are: they can make policy decisions and stick to them. On the other hand, they can be insensitive and remote for exactly the same reason.

Health authorities are responsible to the relevant Secretary of State for purchasing health care for the community within their area of geographical responsibility. They are a recent creation (1995) and combine the functions of the former Family Health Service Authorities and District Health Authorities. They range in size, although much less so than the local authorities with which they must work. The NHS and local government were never completely conterminous, but the recent changes to health authority boundaries, in some cases, and local government, in many others, has made the situation a great deal worse. Two, by no means isolated, examples illustrate the point.

Until 1996, Gwent District Health Authority and Gwent County Council in southeast Wales covered exactly the same area. Gwent Health Authority now covers an area served by five new unitary local authorities. To add a further twist, the health authority and one of the new local authorities have taken over an area which was formerly a part of another county and another health authority.

Kent County Council serves an area covered by two health authorities, East and West Kent. In 1998 the metropolitan area of the county will become Medway, a separate unitary local authority. From then on East Kent Health Authority will cover Medway and part of Kent. The remainder of Kent will continue to be covered by West Kent Health Authority.

Why does this matter? When health and local authorities serve different communities any negotiation between them has to begin by agreeing a target population for the subject under discussion. It is no longer pre-determined by their boundaries. Consider the consequence for a large authority reaching an agreement with a smaller authority which covers only part of its area. A health authority agrees with local authority *A* to handle something in a particular way. Having done so, it is going to be heavily biased towards the same solution in its negotiations with local authority *B*. If local authority *B* insists on a different solution the health authority will have to have two different policies in different parts of its area, and they may have uneven resource implications which are difficult to justify. It is a complication which everyone could live without!

Services and trusts

The NHS trusts provide community and hospital services to patients. They do not cover pre-determined areas like the health authorities. Instead they contract with them to provide a range of services. There is nothing to stop a trust contracting with two or more authorities to provide the same or different services for each. Equally, there is nothing to stop a health authority from contracting with two trusts to provide the same service in, say, the east and west of the authority area. Although their contracts with the health authorities usually relate to a particular area, trusts are not bound by geography (except in the practical sense) and can bid to provide services anywhere.

Trusts vary a great deal in size and in the range of services they provide. They run hospitals, singly or in groups and also provide community services like mental health nursing, district nursing and paramedical services. The trusts are not privatised services. Their assets are wholly owned by the NHS on whose behalf they compete with each other. In the end they are accountable to the secretary of state in the same way as the health authorities.

The patterns of service provision to which all this gives rise vary enormously. In Cornwall for example, no doubt for reasons of geography, the profile could scarcely be simpler: one (county) local authority, one health authority, one community NHS trust and one hospital NHS trust. However, the situation can be, and usually is, a great deal more complicated. One trust in Wales, for example, is responsible for providing community child nursing and the administration of the clinics throughout a (local authority) area. It is also responsible for providing children's clinical (medical) services in half the area. Clinical services in the other half of the area are provided by a different trust.

The more complex the pattern of provision and commissioning, the more difficult it is to accommodate the interests, and coordinate the efforts, of the local authorities, the health authorities and the NHS trusts. Negotiating skills of a very high order are necessary to find pathways through the jungle of competing interests. Above all, it is vital to remember that the final beneficiary of all this effort is the same group of people.

Primary care

GPs are independent contractors with the NHS and have been since its formation. They are now resourced and serviced by the new health authorities but, until the most recent reorganisation in 1995, they had their own separate administrative authorities.

The GPs' traditional rôle has been diagnosis, prescription, treatment and, where necessary, referral for specialist advice and treatment, and they have also had a responsibility for preventive medicine and in health promotion. In recent years these last two activities have increased considerably. Until very recently, however, GPs had no responsibility to ensure that specialist treatment was available nor to purchase it.

The introduction of GP fund-holding

Perhaps the most radical development in the NHS has been the introduction of fund-holding GPs.

> They purchase a range of services which include most routine surgery, outpatient and specialist nursing care. From April 1996 fundholding will be expanded to enable fundholders to purchase elective surgery. A few very large practices will pilot buying all the community, secondary and emergency care their patients need. Some smaller practices purchase a limited range of services, including most community health services but excluding all hospital treatment. Quoted from *A Guide to the National Health Service*, NHS Executive 1995, p.20.

Fund-holding GPs are still in a minority and there has been much controversy about the balance of resources available to them as compared to GPs who are not fund-holders. However, there is no doubt that GPs will become increasingly important as resource allocators within the NHS.

> Primary care should also receive an appropriate share of overall NHS resources, reflecting its growing contribution to health care. Movement of services from secondary to primary care and getting the balance of resources right as a result is a key issue. Quoted from *Primary Health Care: the Future*, NHS Executive, June 1996.

The argument in favour of this development is that GPs are closer to the communities they serve than the other components of the NHS. In addition, patients have a genuine choice of which GP to register with. Even though the great majority now work in group practices it is possible to choose between three or four practices within reasonable reach in all but the most sparsely populated areas. Certainly they are the 'shop front' of the system which almost everyone knows and relates to in some way.

Whatever the force of the positive argument, there is no doubt that it will make the health and social services negotiator's life more difficult. Consider, for example, the brokering of an interagency agreement about, say, a joint approach to child protection or services for elderly people. Formerly, the negotiators drew an area on a map which fell within the boundaries covered by their agencies. They then reached agreement with, or more usually for, the community within that area. GPs, on the other hand, have patient lists rather than boundaries on maps. There might well be four group practices in a smallish town all of which draw patients from every part of the town. So the four practices must agree among themselves what line they wish to take about health-related issues and the use of their resources before they can begin to negotiate with the relevant agencies in the hope of achieving a significant impact. The final outcome might be better and reflect the aspirations of the community more directly but it will certainly be harder to arrive at it.

Size

Whatever the arguments about the level of resources, the size of the NHS is huge, and in the United Kingdom as a whole it spends annually more than £40 billion. What has this got to do with the negotiator? Not much to be frank. If you are from outside it is helpful to know how much the team you are meeting has to spend or manage. But don't be overawed by the huge edifice which stands behind them: they are not negotiating for the whole of it!

An overview of social services

Purpose

In general the services are there to remove, reduce or alleviate a social problem which exists because of a need, a disability or a condition. Quoted from *An Overview of Social Services for Members*, Social Services Strategic Planning, 1996.

You will not find a national mission statement for social services such as the one quoted for the NHS (page 105) because each local authority is autonomous under the law. But most authorities do produce statements of their own and if you are about to negotiate with one of them it is a good idea to obtain and study theirs.

Some people, indeed many people in the social services themselves, believe that the agenda is completely set by the government. It controls the legislation, the guidance (most of which is mandatory), and the level of spending. Certainly the more you know about what the law imposes on authorities in relation to the subject under discussion the better armed you will be. It is also sensible to have some idea about government assumptions about expenditure in your field, but it is not always easy to find out about them. Perhaps the best source of that information is the authority you are negotiating with!

Actually, local authorities have a great deal more discretion and flexibility in the field of social services than they themselves sometimes realise.

- They can decide how far they should target only those in greatest need.

- They have considerable discretion about what they charge for and how much.

- Their global spending is largely dictated to them but they can decide whether it should be biased towards or away from social services.

- They can also decide on the internal balance of expenditure as between, for example, adults and children.

- They can choose how closely they cooperate with others like the health service and other local authorities; how much they buy in and how much they provide directly.

- They can decree the rôle of social services within the authority. At one extreme social services can be strictly a vehicle through which the local authority discharges its legal obligations under social services law; at the other, they can be the coordinator of social governance within the local authority area with an extremely wide community brief.

The more you know about where the particular authority you are talking to stands on these issues, the better. Ask. The questions are perfectly legitimate and they don't weaken your position in any way. Every social services authority produces a community care plan (sometimes called a social care plan) and a children's services plan. They are published documents and most local authorities will let bona fide enquirers have copies without charge. They vary enormously in quality and volume. Sometimes they give a very clear insight into the authority's plans. Sometimes they are little more than a loosely-joined collection of statistics. They always tell you something about the authority and what you are up against when you begin to negotiate with them.

Who are the social services for?

Unlike the NHS the social services are not universal. They are provided for specific groups of vulnerable people. 'Vulnerability' (my word, not the statutory word) is defined in law in various ways, though not, in most cases, very rigorously. There are three main groups of people eligible for social services, all of which contain a number of sub-groups. These are:

1. Vulnerable adults

- mentally ill people,
- people with learning difficulties,
- physically disabled people,
- sensorially disabled people (who are blind, deaf or partially sighted),
- elderly people (by far the largest group),
- people who misuse drugs or alcohol,
- sufferers from HIV/AIDS.

2. Children in need

- children and young people (under 18 years old) who suffer 'significant harm' (physical, sexual or emotional abuse),
- children in social or emotional need,
- children suffering any of the disabilities,
- children under eight years old,
- children and young people in the courts (for whatever reason),
- young people in serious conflict with their parents or carers,
- rootless and homeless young people,
- young people at high risk because of drugs, prostitution or alcohol abuse.

3. Carers and families

- Potentially, anyone who has some responsibility for caring or providing for someone in either of the other two groups, either voluntarily or perforce.

Figure 8.1 gives you an idea of the proportion of total resources devoted to different client groups. (I have deliberately left out the actual figures because they vary a good deal from one authority to another.) If you discover that your local percentage distribution is very different from this, it might provide you with a useful negotiating lever.

Comparative expenditure: social services

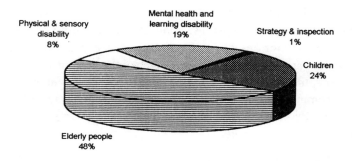

Figure 8.1

It is important to remember the clientele. Social services can only engage you in a meaningful exchange if it concerns one or more of these groups in some way. Homelessness, for example, is not a social services responsibility unless the homeless person also falls within one of the categories in the above list. Exactly the same is true of victims of poverty.

Organisation

We have seen that the local authorities have pretty wide discretion about what social services they provide. When it comes to how they provide them, their discretion is almost total. By law, local authorities must have a designated director of social services, and guidance makes it mandatory in effect for them to have certain posts. One such post which springs to mind is the universal child protection coordinator. Beyond that it is almost impossible to generalise about organisation.

I will risk one generalisation, however: it is almost universal practice now to divide the social services department at very senior level between children's services and adult services. The division is sometimes almost total. I have found it necessary on occasion to talk to a completely different group of people about providing management training (which is of course not specific to one group of clients) in the children's services and in the adult services. One new shadow authority has recently gone for an organisational plan which places children's services with education and adult services with housing.

I can offer very little help in suggesting what you might find in any given authority except to propose, as before, that you ask at an early stage. They will always be happy to provide you with an organisation chart – but it will not always be very helpful. The questions you need to ask about the part of the organisation you are talking to are:

- Is assessment/commissioning/purchasing (all these words are used) functionally separated from direct service provision? Bear in mind that you can't necessarily generalise about this, even within one authority. I know two authorities where these functions (i.e. commissioning and provision) are completely separate commands, both of which are then further split into children's and adult services. That is unusual, but it is quite common to find adult services divided in this way and children's services internally divided by client group (into young children and adolescents, for example).

- Who is going to be making the decision you are interested in if it is not the person you are talking to, and whom, therefore, does he have to convince? If delicately handled that can often be openly addressed. It is useful, for many reasons, to know whether it is a professional or a politician and, if the former, how much expertise she is likely to possess. If you can find out *who* it is as well as *what sort of person* it is so much the better.

Size

Within its own area your social services department is a very big spender indeed. Apart from education, in which the local authority now functions more or less as a distribution centre for schools, it is the biggest spending department in the local authority. As with health, you should not be overawed by the size of it. You are meeting with one team of people, not the whole department.

The other side of the coin is that you cannot assume that communication with one part of a large authority will have any impact on another part. If you do a particularly good job as a provider in the field of children's services the news is more likely to travel to the children's services in neighbouring social services departments than to adult services within the same authority.

Comparisons and conflicts

Clearly health and social services are very different from each other, but their policies are driven by the same secretary of state whose department is the source of most of their money. They are very closely involved with each other in the sense that neither can fulfil many of their statutory or professional functions properly without the active support of the other. On the other hand, that active support has become ever more difficult to achieve with the organisational fragmentation of both services.

Statute and government policy sometimes serve to pull the two sides apart, in spite of ministerial rhetoric exhorting them to work more closely together. The juxtaposition of 'the seamless web of care' with the NHS internal market and social services functional split creates philosophical confusion. The negotiator's real world is often one of deep philosophical inconsistency. It is the practical policies to which both sides must adhere which present the greatest problems.

The NHS has always been, in principle, a free service 'at the point of need'. Every part of the service is free *except those parts which are paid for*. In the case of the social services it has always been the other way round: every part of the service is paid for *except those parts which are free*. As pressure on resources has mounted, this distinction has become increasingly important in the margins between the two services. There the issue tends to be 'Which of us is going to provide this particular service?' It really should be 'How do we each provide the services we provide in ways which support the community?'

There has been a gradual transfer of responsibility from the health service to local authorities for funding 'continuing care'. The cost of looking after patients who no longer require continual medical attention, but who can be cared for in a nursing home environment rather than in hospital, is being increasingly placed upon local authorities.

Increasing pressure on in-patient beds in hospitals produces further tension between the health service and social services. Hospitals need to move patients on when they are recovered and fit for discharge. The patients need appropriate and rapidly provided community care services (they also need community health services, often provided by a different NHS trust). The bed must be made available for a new admission as soon as possible. The system depends on it. This creates further pressure on already squeezed community care resources. These resources are financed by a local authority whose priority is to provide adequate care for elderly, frail and disabled people who are already living in the community.

The crunch comes with 'boundary disputes'. In the past ministers have preferred to leave the two sides to fight it out, keeping themselves relatively free of pressure. They have not given clear guidance about how the boundary should be decided. Skilful negotiation has never been at a greater premium.

Some of the inter-relationships between health and social services may be better understood by looking at Figure 8.2. The activities in the shaded area have most need to communicate on a day-to-day, case-by-case basis. To an extent which varies widely from one place to another these are also the areas which engage in negotiation to achieve a joint strategic plan (which, incidentally, they are legally obliged to do).

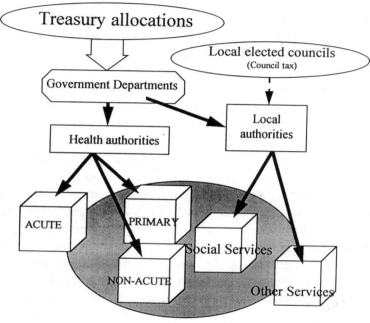

Figure 8.2

The major decision-makers above the shaded area are much more weakly involved with each other. The people in the boxes partly outside the area have other priorities which are not necessarily central to those within the area. In the case of the health service, the acute services are much higher on the 'public anxiety list' than the services in the shaded area. In the case of the local authorities the same is true of education, which is also largely outside the area.

If you are an outsider, from a voluntary organisation or a private service provider for example, you might think that much of the above is irrelevant to you. Remember the negotiating dictum: the more you know about your protagonist, the more powerful your position. Asking about the other side's perception of themselves will usually provide you with illuminating insights into the kind of agency you are dealing with. It will also show them that you are aware of the wider stage and have some understanding of its importance. Almost without exception it will enhance the value of your contribution in their eyes.

Further reading

There is no shortage of literature on the health service. If you go into a bookshop on one of the mainline terminal stations you will almost certainly find an 'ordinary person's guide' of some description on the shelf. However, even in a well-stocked city-centre bookshop you will be fortunate to find a similar book on the personal social services.

Two books which cover the broad spectrum of social services, including health, social security and a good deal else are:

- *Guide to the Social Services*, Family Welfare Association. Published by Waterlow Information Services Ltd. This book is revised annually.

- *Social Services: Made Simple*, by Tony Byrne and Colin Padfield, published by Made Simple Books. The current (fourth) edition was published in 1990.

The first of these is a factual reference book containing up-to-date, but very brief, information. It is no good for gaining a 'feel' of how things work but if you want a quick reference which is as up-to-the-minute as anything can be, this is the book.

The second book is much bigger, more discursive and descriptive. It covers a very broad range of services under the heading 'social' including education and employment. It is an excellent student book and (I find it) very readable. The main drawback is that the current edition is becoming seriously outdated.

Two recent books on, respectively, health and personal social services which you might find interesting are:

- *A Damn Bad Business: The NHS Deformed*, by Jeremy Lee-Potter, published by Victor Gollancz, 1997.

- *The Personal Social Services*, by Robert Adams, published by Longman, 1996.

Both books are critiques of the two services. The first concentrates on the process of reform of the NHS during the past ten years and would be as interesting to an insider as to an external observer. The second is both a description of the services and a critique of them.

Finally, if you just want a (fairly) straightforward description of the NHS you could do worse than read the guide written by the NHS Executive itself: *A Guide to the National Health Service* and available free on the World Wide Web, NHS Executive home page, or by calling 0800 555 777. It is a bit starry-eyed and increasingly out-of-date but a useful brief description for all that.

9. A Common Agenda, a Different Language

Introduction

In this chapter we examine the political and cultural differences between the two services and the impact these have on how decisions are reached.

How decisions are made in local authority social services

Every local authority is different

Local authorities have to obey the law which relates to their activities. Moreover they cannot do *more* than the law mandates them to do. That is what the doctrine of *ultra vires* ('beyond the powers') means. As things stand, discretion in the social services field is extremely wide: social services must, for example, provide a service to a child assessed as 'in need'. However, the authority itself conducts the assessment and therefore has a lot of control over who is judged as being 'in need'. The authority also has wide discretion to decide how to meet the need and how to provide the service. That discretion allows for creative ideas untrammelled by prescriptive legislation, but it also allows for a minimalist response for either political or financial reasons. A very similar range of discretion is present in the adult field.

A number of things militate against too wide a degree of variation however. First, social work is a profession with a common standard of training and qualification; and officers, most of whom are trained social workers, are quite powerful, while not as powerful as doctors in the health service. It is a brave lay person who challenges clinical judgement, however shaky it appears to be. Social work judgement is challenged, occasionally as it relates to an individual client, quite frequently as it relates to policy on how to respond to a recurring situation.

Second, the interpretation of the law is open to challenge in the courts and there have been many successful challenges in recent years. These judgements are carefully weighed in broadsheets and the professional media, but perhaps they do not have quite as much impact on day-to-day practice as is sometimes suggested.

Third, there is more uniformity of expenditure than there used to be because the Government publishes its Standard Spending Assessments (SSAs) for different local authority services. The Government also now provides over 80 per cent of the finance for local government, through a process called the Revenue Support Grant Settlement, and closely controls the freedom of individual authorities to raise more money through local taxation than the Government decides they should.

The new Labour administration has indicated that it will relax these central controls on local government spending in due course. At the time of writing, they remain as they were under the Conservatives.

Member involvement in decisions

It is sometimes claimed that elected members are much too closely involved in practice decisions in social services but leave all the strategic (i.e. political) decisions to the director. This may not be entirely true; but it is not entirely false either! Members pride themselves on being the representatives of their individual constituents and it is difficult for them to find the balance between representing the interests of individuals and exerting unwarranted pressure on their behalf.

The traditional assumption about local government is that elected members make the policies and the officers apply them to individual cases in their everyday administrative work. This stereotype is not quite true for any of the services, but it is particularly misleading in social services. Day-to-day decisions on the majority of individual cases have to be based on professional judgement. Social workers and their managers make assessments of the risks and consequences of different courses of action. They work within policy parameters set by the Social Services Committee, which comprises elected members, and the general framework of resources determined by the local council. Policy guidelines for handling individual cases are not established by elected members, they are developed by professional practice and government guidance, which is itself based on research and the outcome of enquiries and inspections. This guidance has the force of law in effect and is often used in evidence; so the local authority has little option but to accept it.

The strategic decisions which the elected members take are crucial in establishing the general pattern of services in their authority and the priorities for those services. Because they are about abstract issues rather than concrete rules they are difficult to define and tackle. All this makes for a sometimes uneasy and not always appropriate relationship between the rôle of the officers and the rôle of the members.

Outsiders frequently find this incomprehensible and frustrating. NHS staff work in a very different kind of command structure. Voluntary staff usually work in a more flexible framework. Commercial agencies are accustomed to justifying decisions on ethical and commercial grounds only. All of them find the local authority decision-making process difficult to understand.

Unlike some constraints on negotiation, this process is not always something you can establish by straightforward questions. You can usefully find out about the stated policy. 'Any expenditure over £5,000 has to be approved by the committee.' But you need friends at court to interpret the real meaning of such a policy. Does the committee almost always accept the officer's recommendation or does it usually make up its own mind on the day? It is but one example of the need to build the confidence and trust of those you will be negotiating with.

Consider for example the position of a small local voluntary organisation seeking to renew a grant from the local authority. The grant may be used to employ perhaps their only member of staff. They know that the matter will be finally decided by the committee. Do they assume that, barring completely unforeseen circumstances, the agreement they have reached with the officers will be delivered? Or do they assume that they have been engaged in the opening round of a process which will be decided in another place in their absence? Making the right assumption is clearly vital to the way they plan for the negotiation and for the conclusions they draw from it.

On the whole, larger authorities tend to delegate more discretion to officers than small ones, for obvious practical reasons, although some smaller authorities do operate in a highly strategic way, leaving most executive decisions to officers. Often, larger authorities go to considerable lengths to put their members in the front line of day-to-day decisions.

How decisions are made in the NHS

Constitutionally, the NHS could not be more different from the local authorities. Local authorities are apparently free agents, acting as they please within the law, in contrast to the NHS, which is under the direct control of four territorial chief executives who can tell the whole service what it should do. Chief executives can set targets, create a development plan and establish uniform standards throughout. Not only that, but because they are appointed by ministers to implement government policy, and ministers themselves have Cabinet accountability, there is considerable uniformity even across internal national boundaries.

It is not quite like that in either case. As we have seen local authorities are quite heavily constrained in the degree to which they can make independent decisions. The NHS, on the other hand, is such a huge organisation that, if it was managed in the completely top-down way caricatured in the previous paragraph, it would simply grind to a halt.

In any case, the simplistic commercial analogies which bedevilled the debate about both health and social services in the past have given way to wiser counsel. The NHS is not a commercial pyramid but a complex oligarchy comprising not only the secretaries of state and the chief executives, but also the health authorities, the boards of the health trusts and the health policy and health finance divisions of the four departments of state.

It is argued that the changes which have taken place during the past ten years have produced much greater organisational diversity, and a much greater uniformity of standards has been achieved through the issue of more definitive guidance and the application of the patients' charter. I have no way of judging the assertion about standards – there are as many assertions to the contrary – but there is no doubting the truth of the claim of greater organisational diversity.

However, in spite of the operational autonomy of the authorities and trusts and in spite of such mechanisms as local pay bargaining the NHS is still, in many important respects, a unitary national service. Knowledge of how things are done in one health authority or NHS trust is much more likely to be useful in inferring how they might be done elsewhere than is the case with local authorities. All the same, you must be careful not to make too many assumptions when you cross boundaries, especially national ones.

There is real confusion outside the service about the respective rôles of authorities and trusts. Most people understand the principle clearly enough. The authorities commission and finance the service; the trusts provide it. If you want to talk to the NHS about the allocation of its resources you talk to the authority. If you want to talk about the way services are delivered you talk to the relevant trust. From time to time you need to think very clearly indeed about just what you do want. Local authority and other people from outside very often become confused about who is responsible for what, and I venture to suggest that sometimes health service people do too.

It may even be that the Department of Health is not always entirely sure about the structure of the NHS. For example, the Area Child Protection Committees exist to establish standards of practice and effective collaboration among the agencies. Their primary function has always been to coordinate policy and practice rather than to allocate resources. Yet the Department of Health advises that community health interests should be represented by the relevant health authority. I can see the logic of this from the standpoint of geography, but policy and practice are largely determined by the relevant trusts. If I am missing the point here I should be glad of enlightenment.

Common ground

The similarities between health and the local authorities are much greater than the differences, and they are greater still between the non-acute part of the NHS and the social services part of the local authority. The greatest similarity is that they have a largely common clientele and a largely common agenda: their mission is very similar.

The NHS is a universal service and the social services are focused at specific groups. However, those groups also happen to make very heavy demands on the NHS. Consider the hospital and community health services. These are the services provided by the NHS trusts as opposed to those provided by general practitioners and dentists. They represent (very) approximately two-thirds of all NHS expenditure.

To analyse expenditure is difficult, because of the problems in identifying a precise match between expenditure and service detail. Bearing that in mind, I would estimate that perhaps half the hospital and community health services expenditure is on the acute services. The remaining half, except for the maternity service (about 5 per cent of the total), is spent on precisely those people who are also major social services users.

If my calculations are right, about a third of the total NHS expenditure is specifically directed towards elderly people, mentally ill people, young children, and people with learning difficulties – the principal social services target groups. Furthermore, much of the time of general practitioners is taken up by elderly people and young children, and elderly people in particular also make disproportionate demands on the acute services. Taking specific and general services together, perhaps as much as three-fifths of all NHS expenditure is directed towards the social services target groups. Even that is not the end of the story. There is a well-established link between poverty, deprivation and poor health. So it is the most vulnerable members of the general target groups who make disproportionate demands on both services. Taking all these things together the overlapping clientele of the two services is very large indeed.

The purposes for which both health and social services exist are also very similar. They are two of the main devices which society uses to improve the quality of life of those suffering personal misfortune. It is useful to compare the mission statement of the NHS and the summary of the purpose of social services which I quoted in the previous chapter.

The fundamental purpose of the NHS is...greatest possible improvement in the physical and mental health of the people...by promoting health...and caring for those with long term illness and

> disability.... (Alan Langlands, NHS Chief Executive, England; quoted from *A Guide to the National Health Service*, NHS Executive 1995)
>
> In general the services are there to remove, reduce or alleviate a social problem which exists because of a need, a disability or a condition. (Quoted from *An Overview of Social Services for Members*, Social Services Strategic Planning 1996)

Allowing for the different language in which the ideas are expressed, the common ground is well illustrated by these two statements. The social services *agenda* is more comprehensive: a serious illness or disability usually brings in its train a social problem, while a social problem does not necessarily result in illness. By contrast, the health service *clientele* is much more comprehensive: it includes all of us throughout our lives. Nevertheless the central point is the overlapping demand on the two services from the same group of people.

Both services must be accountable for managing their own budgets through their own constitutional command systems. If they take a short-term or excessively narrow view of their responsibilities they will not be able to fulfil their purposes to their full potential and the patient/client will be the loser.

The different meanings of words

All organisations, bureaucracies, professions and services develop their own language. Bureaucracies in particular also develop a code of numbers, initials and acronyms to describe all sorts of things. This is of course potentially very confusing to outsiders, and good negotiators must always be sure that they understand the meaning of the jargon and the codes which are used in discussion and writing. One should never assume that they are being used to obfuscate unless the evidence strongly indicates that. People just become so accustomed to using this kind of shorthand that they are unaware they are doing it. It is always legitimate to ask what something means if you don't know.

There is a second type of jargon, also widely used, the purpose of which is, usually unconsciously, to impress or to disguise vague or imprecise thinking. Its sources are usually management, psychology or, more recently, computer terminology.

> Our indicative budget for future years is in the region of 500K. We will need to undertake an ongoing programme of forward planning, taking account of a number of key parameters. Some of our key players display unconscious avoidance of the necessity to get into this project but if we are going to continue to provide quality assurance to the consumer we will have to do this in the context of detailed monitoring and evaluation of existing services.

I don't need to translate the passage. Most people reading this book will have heard similar verbiage many times. This is not the worst kind of example: the passage does mean *something*. It is quite common to hear passages of speech twice as long as this which mean absolutely nothing.

What do you do when this kind of language crops up as part of an exchange between you and someone in health or social services? (I am taking it as axiomatic that *you* avoid such language yourself.) Having resisted the temptation to poke the speaker in the eye, ask yourself 'Does this mean anything?' Beware! The passage I have quoted does mean something, but if you had heard it spoken you could be forgiven for thinking that it was just verbal padding. You can look at it again in this case to see what the meaning is but, in discussion, you can't usually stop the proceedings, wind back the tape and listen again.

I can only offer you my own device for dealing with this. I go through the following process:

1. I ask myself 'Did I understand that?'

2. If not I say 'I'm sorry, I didn't understand what you just said.'

3. If I do not understand the reprise either I assume that it really has no meaning, so I simply nod.

Incidentally, there is seldom much danger of confusing the two different types of jargon. If you do happen to raise the question in relation to real terminology the answer will almost always be a clarification (unless the concept is very complex or you are very dense!).

The greatest barriers to communication are a few important words which have different meanings, or convey different signals to different groups of people. There are some of these 'barrier words' lying between health and social services. The five I have listed each illustrate a rather different issue.

'The market'

There can be few more important words in the English language just at present than this. It sometimes appears that nothing else matters in the formulation of policy, and it is certainly important in both the health and social services. The problem in this particular case is that it is two different concepts.

The NHS buys many things on the open market, as it always has, but, on the whole, it does not buy in medical care and clinical services: it buys them from itself. There is, however, a very clear division in the NHS between the purchasing arm of the service and the providing arm. The commissioners who work for the health authorities do not provide any kind of direct service. Their rôle is to assess the service requirements of the community they serve and to meet them by 'purchasing' from the NHS trusts.

In order to assess what the community they serve needs, they rely largely on statistical demographic information. There are many output measures which assess value for money, but I do not know how the authorities assess impact and community satisfaction. That is, incidentally, another common factor between health and social services. Activity and throughput are easy to measure, but outcome for the patient/client is usually difficult to assess and even more difficult to measure.

There is also a purchasing rôle for a growing number of budget-holding GPs (who are also service providers themselves), which was, until recently, limited to a narrow range of services. However, a number of practices have been approved to purchase a much wider range of services, and it was the previous government's intention to extend that approval to many more. The way the rôle will unfold is changing rapidly, as we saw in the previous chapter; but there is little doubt that the responsibility for negotiating a range of health (and perhaps other) services will continue to increase.

The change of administration has opened up a number of questions about the future of the internal market concept in the NHS, but so far there are very few answers to report.

'The market' means different things in social services. Most social services departments do not have 'commissioners' in the sense used in the NHS: there are people with that title but they do not operate in the same way. 'Purchasing' in the social services usually means buying services on behalf of individual clients. Care managers make an assessment on behalf of and, preferably, with the client. The care package is then purchased from the providers. In most authorities the purchaser/provider split, by which assessment and care management are functionally separated from service provision, only applies to adult services. Children's services tend to be managed on more traditional client group lines; in other words there is no internal market for children's services. But services for children are purchased from outside the agency just as they are for adults!

The elaborate contractual negotiations in the NHS, by which all services are purchased by the authorities from the trusts, do not take place to the same extent in social services. The price for individual services, for example residential care, is usually rather crudely fixed across the whole sector, taking limited account of variations in quality and degree of intensity. Sometimes there is no reference to any consideration other than the unit cost paid in the previous year, with an allowance for inflation. The services are then purchased, usually on the basis of 'spot' contracts, both internally and from the commercial and voluntary sectors.

Ardent free marketeers and planned economy devotees alike might wonder why things are organised thus. One part of the public service has an elaborate process merely to purchase from itself; another, closely related, part has sometimes no real 'process' at all to purchase from an outside market! The main issue for us is that very often the people inside both systems do not realise that such differences exist.

'Community'

This word is the cause of many misconceptions with which communication between the health and social services, and indeed much of the rest of the public service, is shot through. Sometimes it is used to indicate identity of interest, function or condition: 'the nursing community', 'the black community'. Sometimes it describes a geographical group, as in 'the Docklands community'. It is used in that sense by health authorities to describe their purchasing rôle 'on behalf of the community'. The word 'community' is a factotum and is often used as verbal padding. I have recently seen in print 'The world community', 'the student community' and 'the sheltered-housing-complex community'. I think that what is meant is 'people', 'students' and 'residents'. Only the last of the three requires any other qualification.

This is not merely a diatribe against the lazy use of 'community'. The trouble with this particular word is that it appears in health and social services language – sometimes in usage, sometimes in law – with many different meanings. 'Community Home', 'The NHS and Community Care Act 1990' and 'Community Service Order' are all legal phrases with quite different meanings. 'Community Home' is, in reality, a local authority children's home (i.e. an institution); a 'Community Service Order' is a court sentence for a crime; and in some high profile mental health cases recently 'community care' means no care at all.

When used to express warm and positive concepts (like community development and community care) it is often imprecise to the point of meaninglessness. When used to express precise ideas (like community service and community tax) it takes on punitive, coercive or controlling overtones. Negotiators need to make quite sure that the word is being used and understood in the same sense by everyone round the table.

'Partnership'

This word has a definite meaning in both the health and social services – unfortunately the meanings are different! In the social services field the word means 'working in collaboration with the client'; in the health service it means 'working together in an equal professional relationship'. One might assume that, as the word has such different senses, there would be little room for misunderstanding. Don't believe it.

I was present at an extraordinarily tense meeting between the two disciplines, during which the word flew backwards and forwards across the table, comprehensively misunderstood on each occasion. We suddenly realised what the problem was and it was like taking the cork from a bottle.

The lesson to draw from this is not to be afraid of seeming stupid if you ask for clarification about something. Most people are not stupid. If they seem so to you one quite plausible explanation is that what you are hearing is not what they are saying. They may be speaking a slightly different language; and it is the 'slightly' which is the operative word. My son went as an exchange student to the United States. On his first day in school there he asked the girl sitting next to him if she could lend him a rubber. Neither of them knew that the English word for eraser was the same as the American word for condom!

'Professional'

'Professional' has a range of meanings. Doctors tend not to use the word to imply professional competence, preferring instead 'clinical'. The word 'clinical' has an air of detached disinterest. Such judgements are based, so it sometimes appears to be implied, on an almost mystical body of knowledge, skill and experience to which no one outside the profession (the noun is quite often used) can possibly aspire. Doctors are usually quite secure in their supremacy, no doubt with good reason in relation to actual clinical judgement. A problem sometimes occurs, however, when the habitual supremacy spills over the 'clinical' boundary and into the murkier waters of policy development or, worse still, into the area of someone else's 'professional competence'.

Nurses, social workers and, beyond the remit of this book, teachers sometimes tend to be prickly about their 'professional' judgements. They are less secure in their power bases than the doctors. Many individuals envy the doctors' greater professional authority and for some this comes out as hostility.

In the social services field most senior managers and administrators are qualified social workers, but in the NHS the position is more mixed. Many managers in the NHS are professionally trained nurses or doctors, but many are not. They are all 'professionally' trained as NHS managers and use the word to mean 'competent, disciplined and disinterested' as managers. Because the non-medical professions tend to be rather sensitive about their 'professional' territory, they sometimes resent the use of the word by others.

The problem with words like 'community' and 'partnership' is confusion of meaning, but the problem with 'professional' is territory. 'Professional jealousy' can act as a serious obstruction to effective communication and negotiation.

'Patient/client'

The problem with these two words is not what they mean but the underlying assumptions which people make about the relationship between patients/clients and the various professionals: what others see of us is seldom what we see of ourselves and this relationship illustrates this more starkly than most.

Social workers are seen by some sections of the public and the media as little better than body snatchers. They exercise arbitrary power and control over children, families and vulnerable people without professional restraint. Social workers, see themselves, by contrast, as working in partnership with clients, respecting their confidentiality and relating to them in a non-judgemental way. They promote equal opportunities and do not exercise arbitrary power.

The public image of nurses, on the other hand, is very positive, and they are usually portrayed as warm and caring, if rather passive. They see themselves positively as well, of course, but tend to regard their relationship with patients as more directive and less passive than the public image. They consider themselves more willing to take difficult and unpopular decisions in the best medical interests of the patient than is generally perceived.

Doctors also have a positive public image but it is more guru-like than most of them would prefer. Many of them see themselves in much the same way as social workers see themselves: as people who explain the options to, and agree the best decision with, the patient.

What can the negotiator working with these professionals infer from this?

- Unless you are a member of the same professional group you are unlikely to share the same perception of their relationship with their (and probably also your) clientele.

- The (even well-informed) public perception is almost certainly something of a caricature and sometimes a complete inversion of reality.

- Their own idealised assumptions about their relationship with their clientele are likely to be somewhat at variance with the practical realities.

In short, you need to tread carefully. If you ride roughshod over your protagonist's self-perception they will be alienated and mistrustful.

Perceived differences in professional values

The NHS and the social services are organised in very different ways, as we have already seen. It is stating the obvious to point out the different skills and knowledge required by social workers, nurses, doctors and the different paramedical professions. When we are feeling vulnerable and insecure we tend to hide behind these differences. Our professional standards are in some way higher than theirs. How can we trust them with confidential information? How can we hope to explain in five minutes, across a negotiating table, things which have taken us a professional lifetime to acquire? Better just to keep them in ignorance so they can do little damage. 'A little knowledge is a dangerous thing.'

The striking thing about these enormous professional differences is that they usually evaporate once trust is firmly established. Issues like confidentiality and the sharing of information can be resolved by the practical application of jointly agreed principles. That is not to say that the practicalities are not themselves sometimes difficult, but, in my experience, agreeing the principles never is, once trust is established.

The same is true of professionals outside the two large organisations. Because they run an old people's home or work for a children's voluntary organisation they do not change their professional spots. This group is different in one important respect. Most health and social care professionals working outside the public bureaucracies have had bureaucratic experience themselves. GPs have had hospital experience, social workers almost always start their career in the public or the large voluntary service, and nurses have always had hospital and very probably community health experience. They all know, even if only in the distant past, what it is like to work within a large organisation.

The reverse is usually not true. Professionals and managers who have only ever worked in large public service bureaucracies usually have little idea about the constraints which operate in a small business. It is not the often commented, but usually spurious, commercial/not-for-profit dichotomy which causes the trouble. Small enterprises, whether charitable or commercial, can respond very quickly and flexibly because they do not have to negotiate decisions with a large internal constituency. On the other hand, they usually operate on small margins and tight timescales. It is a major problem for both sides during negotiation. The small enterprise needs to respond quickly or go out of business. The bureaucracy needs time to achieve internal consent and ownership.

Budgeting and accounting: different timescales and processes

From time to time the financial process and timescale becomes important to the negotiator. Knowing something about how it works is always useful and sometimes crucial. At the end of the financial year, for example, an underspent agency can be very eager to purchase services or (especially) capital equipment. They may be willing to pay some or all of the bill upfront. An overspent agency will only spend what it cannot avoid and will delay payment if it can.

It is useful to know where in the financial planning cycle the people on the other side of the table are at different times of the year. Unfortunately one of life's little difficulties, and a source of some friction between the two, is that these cycles are different for the NHS and the local authorities. They both work to the same financial year as each other (and the rest of the public sector) beginning 5 April. But the timing of the critical decisions is different. To understand why, it is best to begin at the top.

The whole process begins each year in June when a round of consultations (which are of course negotiations) starts within the spending ministries. Over the next eight months they involve their service providing agencies (the quangos, the armed forces, the Benefits Agency, the NHS, the local authorities and many others). Around the end of July the first written submission of spending proposals goes to the Treasury.

During the course of September and October the pace becomes increasingly frenetic as the Chief Secretary to the Treasury and the spending ministers engage in a series of bilateral meetings and civil servants haggle behind the scenes. The budget which is the outcome of all this is held in November and the Chancellor of the Exchequer announces his spending decisions. At that time he advises the spending ministries of their allocations for the coming financial year, although fine tuning continues into December.

A feature of this process which strikes many foreign observers as extraordinary is that it is a single year decision. The annual public expenditure survey does look three years ahead and produces indicative budgets, but they are not binding and can only be used as planning indicators. Because of that all public expenditure is year-on-year.

The Whitehall Ministries (in our case of course the important one is the Department of Health) receive their allocations in relation to their main spending programmes and they cannot move resources from one programme to another without Treasury consent. The territorial departments, the Scottish, Welsh and Northern Ireland Offices, receive a global sum (called the 'block vote') for all the services for which they are responsible. They have much more freedom to decide how to distribute it internally.

The spending assessments on which the Treasury allocates a sum to cover the cost of the health and social services are based on negotiations with the English Department of Health. The Standard Spending Assessments which result are published in England. The local authorities are free to spend their allocation as they decide, although the publication of the SSAs puts them under considerable pressure to stay broadly within those guidelines. Within several political and procedural constraints the Secretaries of State for Scotland, Wales and Northern Ireland are much freer to distribute their block votes as they see fit.

Shortly before Christmas, or early in January, the four departments tell the health authorities what they will be allocated during the coming year. Again there is some fine tuning to be done, and the authorities are lucky to learn exactly what they will have to spend before the end of January at the earliest.

On the same timescale, the Secretaries of State are also announcing their allocations for local authority social services spending. These will form the part of the Revenue Support Grant settlement (the RSG) which will be paid to each local authority.

Up to this point the timing of expenditure decisions for health and social services has been identical, but now the processes begin to diverge. When the local authorities receive the RSG decision it only represents about 80 per cent of what they need to spend. They then have to decide on the level of council tax they will need to raise in order to make up the balance. They have limited discretion about this. If they exceed Government guidelines they will be 'capped' to force them to spend overall no more than the Government thinks fit.

In spite of these limits, the council tax decision still has to be made. Only when it has will the authority know the size of its overall budget for the coming year, and only then can it begin to decide how much each of its departments will have to spend. Each of these decisions needs the ratification of the council following the same kind of negotiations which have accompanied every stage of this process.

The Social Services Director will not know definitely what her budget will be until late February at the earliest. It is not unknown for that decision to be made *after* the financial year to which it relates has begun.

Meanwhile the health authorities are beginning to firm up decisions with the NHS trusts with which they are intending to contract in the knowledge of the spending levels they will be able to achieve. Since the introduction of the contracting process, this has become much more drawn-out than previously, and contracts are not usually signed until well into the financial year to which they relate. Figure 9.1 summaries the process I have described.

This can present huge problems when the two organisations are engaged in joint planning, either between themselves or in relation to third parties. You can see from the above that a social services department might be running about two months or more *behind* the health authority with which it is discussing resource allocation, but it might be about two months *ahead* of an NHS trust with which it is discussing processes. However, like all obstacles, this one becomes more tractable the better it is understood. At the very least, understanding will prevent the frustration developing into mutual recrimination.

An area of particular conflict

It is usually at the boundaries of responsibility that tensions between public bodies are at their greatest, or where their objectives appear to be in conflict with one another. In the case of the health and social services the former is much more

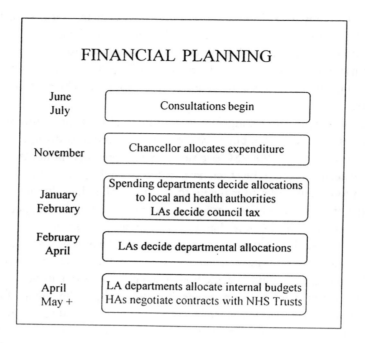

FINANCIAL PLANNING

June July	Consultations begin
November	Chancellor allocates expenditure
January February	Spending departments decide allocations to local and health authorities LAs decide council tax
February April	LAs decide departmental allocations
April May +	LA departments allocate internal budgets HAs negotiate contracts with NHS Trusts

Figure 9.1

common than the latter. A single item has recently come to dominate the agenda of unresolved issues. In the terminology of the trade it is called 'continuing care'. Unless you are actually involved in this (in which case you will be acutely aware of the details) you need only understand the issue in principle. The conflict has become so powerful in some areas that it has tainted the whole relationship between the two organisations.

In essence, the social services department and its corresponding health authority have to agree a social care plan and to coordinate their resource management together. One aspect of this is that they have to agree a boundary definition. At what point does the social services department take over responsibility for providing care for the (for all practical purposes, elderly) patient when he leaves hospital?

This is, of course, an expensive service for both the health and the social services agencies. In a case like this, the patient/client will need substantial care or convalescence. At what point in the balance between treatment and care should the social services department take over? Both agencies are accountable to their respective authorities for providing the service for which they are responsible as economically as possible, but conflict between them is counter-productive to the interests of the patient/client. The money for both services comes largely from the same ultimate source: all the more imperative to achieve a workable agreement.

The difficulty is that the two agencies have no basis on which they can make a rational decision at local level, and there is no arbiter. Government advice in the form of circulars is imprecise: the local agencies are enjoined to cooperate. It is like a game of football with no referee and in which both sides are expected to win! The level of maturity and skill required to reach agreement under such circumstances is very high, but failure to do so is damaging to the interests of both organisations and the people they serve.

Information and communication

Health and social services have a large overlap of clientele and many objectives in common. You might conclude that their information needs have much in common, and you would be right. A few health authorities have managed to join forces with their social services counterparts to design a common database. There are a few databases of elderly people and the services they require, managed by one agency on behalf of both, for example. The advantages of doing that are substantial.

- There are significant savings in systems management.
- There is a common basis on which to conduct a dialogue.
- Joint research into the demographics of need and patterns of service distribution is greatly simplified (and thus, once more, much cheaper to conduct).
- Finally, and in some ways most importantly of all, the electronic network which it is necessary to establish provides a communication link between the two agencies and the people within them.

Both health and social services manage their client/patient and service records using a variety of electronic database systems. These systems are usually designed by software houses specialising in this kind of database, although sometimes they are devised by internal IT services. They are nearly always built on one of a small number of database platforms supplied commercially by the software giants of the computer industry such as Microsoft™ and Lotus™. The thing that the non-technical person (like me) needs to understand is that these database systems are, or can easily be made, technically compatible. The collaboration referred to in the previous paragraph is rarely achieved in practice.

There are two issues here for the negotiator. Most obviously, information management may become the subject of negotiation itself. More generally, the more that information of mutual interest is shared using a common language and standards, the more likely the negotiation is to be successful.

Part III

10. Exercises in Negotiation

Introduction

This final part of the book is intended primarily for facilitators and trainers. It contains a number of simulation exercises which have been used by Pi Associates, to whom I am indebted for permission to reproduce them, and my own agency SSSP. If you are intending to participate in a learning session in which one of these exercises is used *don't read it until the exercise is finished* – the whole point is lost if you do.

Exercise A is self-explanatory. The remaining three exercises each comprise three short papers: a general brief for both sides and a separate brief for each side in the simulation. If you are facilitating, once you read through them you will readily grasp the point. You can use them as they are for simulation exercises or as templates to construct exercises more immediately relevant to your own needs. The substance is kept to a deliberate minimum. Participants should be instructed to be creative and use their additional knowledge of the situation.

EXERCISE A What's special about us?
(What are our unique selling points?)

Purpose

This exercise has two purposes. It can be used as a general introduction and as a preamble to a simulation which is based more closely on reality. It is also designed to give the group as a whole an opportunity to think systematically about what is really special about them as individuals and as a team.

The scenario

The whole group at the seminar has decided to leave the agency and set up an independent service. You will manage and run a high quality service for whoever wishes to buy it from you. Your big chance has just arrived. Crazy County Council/Health Authority has just announced its intention to tender for running the service in the north of its area as a pilot for the whole authority. It's a big job but you think you can do it. Why should they give the tender to you?

Process

There are four phases: individual rankings, small group rankings (three or four in a group), whole group negotiation and debriefing. Each is described in a little more detail in Figure 10.1.

Phase	Time	Description
INDIVIDUAL RANKINGS	15 minutes	From figure 10.2 decide yourself which *five* 'unique selling points' should be given the highest priority in promoting the service you can provide to the community. You may want to list more than five points: don't! This is about identifying the most important issues; not all the issues. You may want to add issues which are not included. You can add up to two more if you like but only by sacrificing an equal number on the list. Space is included at the bottom of figure 10.2 if you want to use it.
SMALL GROUP RANKINGS	45 minutes	Working together you should negotiate which *five* points should be given the highest priority. You should identify a spokesperson for the group who will take the lead for the group in the whole group negotiation. You should help your negotiator to prepare for the negotiation. Use the matrix (figure 5.1) to think about your desired and minimum outcome, your strengths and weaknesses and the position the other groups might take. And think about tactics.
THE NEGOTIATION	60 minutes	The spokesperson will now represent your group in the final three/four-way negotiation using the strategy and tactics you have agreed. **Only the spokesperson may negotiate** but she/he may seek an adjournment at any stage to confer with the group about line to take if that seems to be necessary. You will have decided which five points you want and which you are not prepared to sacrifice at any cost (your minimum acceptable). The remaining members of the small groups observe their representative closely. The most useful learning from this phase is to note what seems to be working and why.
DEBRIEFING	15/20 minutes	What happened; what skills were used; what can be learned.

Figure 10.1

What's special about us?

Choose only five things from the following list (or add your own)

A unique selling point is a characteristic of the service you offer which distinguishes you from others who provide similar services. If you find the marketing jargon distasteful simply choose another phrase. It is the concept which is important.

Don't forget that you are looking for the five things which make you special *to them*.

A.	Speed of response; we are always there when the client needs us
B.	Continuity and follow up; ongoing support
C.	Well established as a group; liaison network with other agencies
D.	'A listening service'; special attention to the views of the community
E.	Well qualified team
F.	Smooth processes of care management: introduction/ assessment/ planning/ ongoing care/intervention
G.	Comprehensive range of supports for clients/patients and their families
H.	Services not expensive
I.	Top priority given to confidentiality
J.	'We go where the need is'
K.	Intimate knowledge of resources for this service
L.	Flat hierarchical structure
M.	Fairness and social justice a high priority
N.	Up to date training and development
O.	A very high standard of service
P.	Very flexible; responsive to changing needs of clients/patients and the client authority
Q.	Top priority given to equal opportunities
R.	Top priority given to race awareness among staff
S.	Very experienced team
T.	"We deliver: we always keep our promises"
U.	Team are highly skilled negotiators on their clients/patients behalf
V.	Our aim is a high quality service
W.	An excellent backup service (won't bother you with 'little local difficulties')
X.	Or
Y.	Or

Figure 10.2

© Pi Associates 1997

EXERCISE B Voluntary and statutory agencies

Briefing for negotiation B – both teams

This exercise involves negotiating an agreement for the continuation of an existing project between two new unitary authorities and a team representing a voluntary agency.

The scenario

There is in existence a formally negotiated agreement between the former county authority and the agency, which is due to expire at the beginning of the coming April. There is an agreement between the two successor authorities to finance existing projects (including this one) on the basis of a 65/35 per cent split for one year only, also ending at the beginning of the coming April.

After many months of discussion, starting well before reorganisation was implemented and originally involving an officer, now retired, from the county, the two authorities have finally agreed to meet with the agency team to try to establish the basis of a future agreement. It is this meeting you will be preparing for and conducting.

The common ground is that the project costs a total of £150,000 per annum and employs six staff. It is currently funded to the tune of £45,000 by the agency, £68,000 by the larger authority and £37,000 by the smaller. The project operates for the moment, rent-free, from accommodation which the larger authority has inherited from the county. Officers from both authorities are well pleased with the quality of the service which has been provided in the past. It is no secret that they are operating in a climate of great uncertainty and never know, from one decision to the next, which way members will jump. The known starting point for all participants in the negotiation is that, all things being equal, a way should be found to keep the project on track.

Of course all things are not equal.

Your brief

You will also receive an additional briefing which provides some information about the agreement to be negotiated. It is not very detailed, which gives you lots of latitude in your negotiations. The purpose of the simulation is to allow practice in negotiation skills. The simulation does not pretend to replicate the real world in every respect. You should, therefore, make common-sense assumptions where necessary.

Briefing for negotiation B – the local authority team

N.B. This part is known only to your team.

Your starting point is that you want this negotiation to succeed. Both authorities recognise at officer level that the unit has done a good job and that it needs to remain intact if it is to be viable. The authorities' member perspective is rather different: the Chair and Deputy Chair in both authorities are completely agreed that they want to function independently of all outside services from whatever source and, above all, independently of each other! Ideally, they would like simply to take over the relevant proportion of the unit, but you have managed to convince them (almost) that to do so would result in a poorer service at greater cost.

You have had a considerable struggle to convince your members to continue to support the unit after the year's moratorium and the struggle is by no means over. Resources are very constrained for the current year and there is nothing to suggest that life will get easier.

In order to carry support forward in the authority you are convinced that you need to achieve agreement that, at the very most, the local authority contribution will be no greater than it is now and that the level of service will remain the same. You also know that there is no chance of convincing the committee that support should be committed, at this stage, for longer than one further year.

Most importantly, you need some good ammunition to include in the report to demonstrate convincingly that it is a first-rate project run at reasonable cost. There is some feeling, not only among members, that the agency style is rather Rolls Royce for today's hard world. Within the social services, people are heard to say that they would like to be able to make the same investment in staff training and have the same protected workload.

P.S. There is an unfortunate side issue to be deal with rather tactfully. The director elect of the smaller authority said some months ago (at Christmas – at a party!) to the divisional director of the agency that he hoped to be able to discuss an 'expanded rôle' for the unit and to second one or two staff to it to make this happen. Fortunately, he was not very specific about what he had in mind because it has since become completely apparent (and should have been at the time) that it is a political non-starter. The two authorities know this and the agency should have been disabused long ago, but somehow nobody has quite got round to telling them.

Do not share this briefing with participants who will be representing the agency.

Briefing for negotiation B – the agency team

N.B. This part of the paper is known only to your team.

Your starting point is that you want this negotiation to succeed as a basis on which a new three-year agreement can be reached. You have a high investment in being able to reach an understanding with your local authority colleagues which you are fairly sure you can deliver on behalf of the agency.

Funding to the tune of 30 per cent on current figures is in line with the agency's current policy. On the other hand this is a 'statutory' service which the local authorities would have to provide if you did not. There is a strongly held view in some powerful quarters inside the agency that such services should be provided more or less at the expense of the local authorities. There is also an increasing squeeze on the divisional budget, which you have a responsibility to ease where you can.

You are concerned that Head Office is 'moving the goalposts'. From next financial year onwards there will be a management cost of 12 per cent added to the overall notional budget. This will be added to the agency contribution, thereby taking it above 30 per cent. To make your life yet more difficult you have been unable to discover whether the 12 per cent is to be calculated on the £150,000 total cost or the £45,000 agency contribution.

The director of one of the two authorities (the smaller) has intimated informally that not only does his authority wish the project to continue, it wishes it to assume a rather ill-defined 'wider rôle' in its patch and is willing to place a social worker on secondment to increase the professional resources of the team. You are happy for that to happen, but only if it is clear that the additional task makes no more demands than the one additional worker: the team is already under some pressure.

Your 'bottom line' for the partnership to continue is that there should be no reduction in the local authorities' financial contribution for next year, and, of course, no reduction in the standard of service you offer. You recognise that that is all you may succeed in getting until things settle down, but you are not willing to settle for that level of payment beyond the first year of the agreement (i.e. beyond next April). This may turn out to be somewhat at odds with your desire to reach a three-year agreement.

Do not share this briefing with participants who will be representing the local authorities.
© SSSP 1997

EXERCISE C The public and private sectors

Briefing for negotiation C – both teams

This exercise involves negotiating a basic agreement for residential and nursing care between a local authority team and a team representing the local nursing homes and care homes associations.

The scenario

The former county authority had set (rather than negotiated) a basic price it would pay for residential and nursing home beds in the voluntary and independent sectors. Last year it was £210 per week for a residential bed and £310 per week for a nursing home bed. There was little price flexibility to reflect the intensity of support which the resident might need. In an exceptional case a nursing home could negotiate an addition to provide an exceptional level of nursing care, but the option was rarely exercised in practice and did not apply to the residential homes at all.

The director of social services for the new unitary authority has agreed to set the price for the future on the basis of an annual negotiation, provided it includes an agreement about minimum standards as well as price *and provided* that there is one negotiation with the associations representing both residential and nursing care.

Your brief

On the next page is a briefing which provides some information about the agreement to be negotiated. It is not very detailed, which gives you lots of latitude in your negotiations. The purpose of the simulation is to allow practice in negotiation skills. The simulation does not pretend to replicate the real world in every respect. You should, therefore, make common-sense assumptions where necessary.

Briefing for negotiation C – purchasers

(Not to be disclosed to the providers team.)

You are a member of a senior group representing the Social Services Contracts Unit and the Community Care Division meeting a team representing the local nursing homes and care homes associations. This meeting does not have authority to reach a final agreement – both sides will need to seek ratification – but you are eager to reach agreement on the recommendations to go to the authority and the associations without many 'reserved positions' on either side.

Last year's price per bed per week, based on national figures, was £210 in the residential homes and £310 in the nursing homes. You have calculated that you have little flexibility to increase that within budget. You are interested to see what the associations have to offer by way of 'minimum standards' and would be able to find an extra 5 per cent absolute maximum (£221/£326) in return for an acceptable profile of minimum standards which the associations could guarantee would be delivered by all their members.

Your people are working on the production of a minimum standards document based largely on 'Homes Are For Living In'. But it is proving difficult to finalise the consultation paper and you do not want to show too much of your hand at this stage about what it might contain (in fact you do not know!).

You are anxious to improve the 'care in the community' options available to the authority and are interested to hear what the associations have to offer by way of ideas for 'outreach' services (e.g. domestic services or respite care) and at what cost.

Your subtext is that levels of bed take-up will reduce as community services increase.

Briefing for negotiation C – providers

(Not to be disclosed to the purchasers team.)

You are a member of the negotiating team representing the two associations meeting a senior group representing the Social Services Contracts Unit and the Community Care Division. This meeting does not have authority to reach a final agreement – both sides will need to seek ratification – but you are eager to reach agreement on the recommendations to go to the authority and the associations without many 'reserved positions' on either side.

Last year's price per bed per week was £210 residential and £310 nursing. Your brief is to regard those prices as a baseline on which to add additional costs for additional services which individual residents require, on the assumption that an addition to the baseline price will be the norm rather than the exception. You are able to concede a reduction to the baseline by an absolute maximum of 5 per cent (£200/£295) provided that the authority defines that as 'minimum level of care' and that the definition is elaborated in such a way as to make it clear that there will be additional costs for the great majority of residents, based on the care package they require.

You are also anxious to get some assurances about levels of bed take-up during the coming year. Some of your members are experiencing a vacancy level which is putting their livelihood at risk at present.

The director of social services has already made it clear that he wants to see agreement on 'minimum standards' as part of the package. You are anxious to hear what the authority has in mind in addition to minimum standards required for registration.

© SSSP 1997

EXERCISE D An NHS hospital trust

Briefing for negotiation D – general brief

One of the wards for which the business manager has responsibility is thoracic surgery, which is staffed as follows:

- Two ward sisters who work the day and night shifts.

- On day shifts the staff complement is:

  - eight E grades (full-time equivalents), six of which are full-time,
  - eight D grades (full-time equivalents), seven of which are full-time,
  - four nursing auxiliaries (NAs).

- On night shifts the staff complement is:

  - three E grades (full-time equivalents), two of which are part-time,
  - four D grades (full-time equivalents) all of which are part-time,
  - one NA.

The ward has 22 beds, a four-bed high dependency unit (HDU), and a three-room emergency admissions unit (EAU). The current position is that 18 beds are occupied, as are three of the four high dependency beds. There is no one in the emergency admissions unit.

A problem which frequently arises for the business manager and the ward sister is to provide qualified staff cover for the HDU and the EAU.

Briefing for negotiation D – business manager's brief

You are persistently frustrated by staffing problems in the thoracic ward that you believe should be dealt with by the ward sister, especially because she is extremely able and very experienced.

You now believe you have the ideal solution to prevent future problems. You have enough money in the budget to employ one full-time E grade and one full-time D grade in addition to the current staff complement. You feel strongly that they should be full-time appointments.

- Full-time staff create fewer problems for you.

- Appointing full-time staff virtually guarantees that the posts will be retained in the long term.

- Full-time staff are cheaper in terms of overtime, holiday and sickness payments.

- Having full-time staff gives you the flexibility to use them elsewhere, in other wards for example, as and when necessary. It effectively creates an internal staff 'bank'.

You have approximately £27,000 plus 12 per cent overhead costs available for these posts.

You know that the ward sister is unlikely to share your view of the benefits of employing full-time staff. You get on very well with her and do not wish to upset her. You have arranged to meet her to discuss the issue.

Briefing for negotiation D – ward sister's brief

You are persistently having to deal with staffing issues in your thoracic ward, many of which are created by a preponderance of full-time staff who have less flexibility when it comes to covering emergencies. You believe that the business manager now has enough money in the budget to put more staff on the ward and you feel strongly that they should be part-time.

- Part-time staff give you flexibility in meeting emergencies, especially in the HDU and the EAU.

- Full-time staff are often underemployed for long periods during their shifts when things are going smoothly. This could be reduced or eliminated with more part-time staff.

- Good, qualified part-time staff are not too difficult to recruit and, although this means more to manage, you are quite happy with that. Your current part-time staff are excellent and you are delighted with how flexibly they operate.

The business manager has invited you to a meeting to discuss the issue. You anticipate that he will not share your view of the advantages of employing part-time staff. You get on with him very well on a day-to-day basis.

© Pi Associates 1997

11. Key Learning Points

The key learning points from the end of the Introduction and the chapters in Part I are grouped here for convenient reference. They are at the end of the book so that you can cut them out as an *aide-mémoire* if you want, without wrecking the whole book.

Introduction

Be clear what you want

1. Understand the context
2. Prepare the ground
3. Ways of managing and coping
4. Remember: a protagonist is not a competitor.

Preparation

1. Do I have rôle conflicts? Do I need to address my attitude to negotiation? Do I understand competition/negotiation?
2. How much time, effort and commitment should be involved? – Write a time plan.
3. Are we clear and agreed about what we want? – All of us?
4. Do we know what they want?
5. Have we considered secondary issues?
6. Do we know their responsibilities and interests? Who is going to find out about/make use of them?
7. Have we prepared a matrix?

The people context

1. Do we have a 'professional' agenda? – Independent/knowledge-based.

2. Who is watching them? – The constituency.

3. Do they have the power to decide? – Money/policy/practice.

4. What timescales? – Large/small enterprise.

5. What is the financial agenda? – Profit and loss or budget/procedure?

6. What are the external factors? – Political or economic?

The organisation context

1. The public sector is driven by political priorities rather than financial efficiency. You need to be aware of their underpinning values and to be clear where you stand on them.

2. The language of public sector priorities is as important as the priorities themselves. You should use it when you negotiate with them.

3. The primary purpose of the commercial sector is to make money, but they place no less value on standards and quality than the other two sectors.

4. There are different implications in being paid by salary (i.e. by time) and by fee (i.e. by output).

5. The public and voluntary sectors have their own agenda and priorities. They must both be willing to pay to see them included in the outcome. It is not a straightforward of client/provider relationship between them.

Strategy and tactics

1. Do you know what you want?

   No = decide.
   Yes = move on to the next question.

2. Do you know your bottom line?

   No = read through the key issues again.
   Yes.

3. Do you know what they want?

   No = research/network/ASK.

   Yes.

4. Are you clear about timing?

   No = read through the key issues again.
   Yes.

5. Are you clear about money?

   No = don't be coy – what do you want/need?
   Yes.

6. Have you planned your tactics?

   No = read through the key issues again.
   Yes.

People talking

1. Messages – listen for the signals as well as the substance.

2. Emotional outbursts – stay calm and unemotional, but don't patronise.

3. Are we trying to establish the same kind of relationship? Is the same message being received as the one which is being sent, especially, but not only, between men and women?

4. Skills – don't forget all the skills you already possess (although you may need to work at applying them).

Obstacles and opportunities

1. Make the most of the language and perceptions you share with your protagonists: don't forget they represent a different 'side' from you.

2. Work together to meet the needs of both your constituencies, but don't be tempted to collude against them.

3. If you go 'over their heads' you may lose more than you gain. Careful preparation may achieve the same ends without provoking hostility.

4. Don't exploit their weakness: it probably isn't right and it probably isn't effective!

5. If your protagonist uses power tactics to gain advantage, remember that he needs you: don't respond by adopting the inferior rôle.

6. Learn to manage your own particular kind of panic.

7. If you lose your way in negotiation stop until you find it again or let a colleague take the lead.

Bibliography

Adams, R. (1996) *The Personal Social Services*. London: Longman.

Burchfield, R.W. (ed) (1996) *Fowler's Modern English Usage*. Oxford: Oxford University Press.

Byrne, T. and Padfield, C. (1990) *Social Services: Made Simple*, fourth edition. London: Made Simple Books.

Concise Oxford English Dictionary (1996) Oxford: Oxford University Press.

Family Welfare Association (1997) *Guide to the Social Services*, 85th edition. Waterlow Information Services Ltd.

Fisher, R. and Ury, W.L. (1982) *Getting to Yes*. London: Hutchinson.

Hart, R. (1996) *Effective Networking for Professional Success*. London: Kogan Page.

HMSO (1997) White Paper on Social Services – Achievement and Challenge.

Karrass, G. (1986) *Negotiate to Close*. London: HarperCollins.

Lee-Potter, J. (1997) *A Damn Bad Business: the NHS Deformed*. London: Victor Gollancz.

NHS Executive (1995) *A Guide to the National Health Service*. London: Department of Health.

NHS Executive (1996) *Primary Health Care*. London: Department of Health.

Social Services Strategic Planning (1996) *An Overview of Social Services for Members*. Unpublished resource document to accompany a seminar. Local Government Management Board.

Tannen, D. (1991) *You Just Don't Understand: Men and Women in Conversation*. London: Virago.

Thorn, J. (1991) *How to Negotiate Better Deals*. Didcot: Mercury.